To Amy,
  Thank you for your
contributions to empowering
women! Stephanie Jenkins

RED
FLAGS

D0937321

Stephanie Jenkins, MSW

ISBN: 979-8-9852235-0-7

DEDICATION

This book is dedicated to all the women who have ever felt shattered and broken from a manipulative and toxic relationship. My heart extends to you. You are wiser and stronger than you think. I pray this book helps you live a bold, free life.

And to my children, who were the initial motivation for me writing this book. I pray you have a lifetime of healthy, loving relationships.

CONTENTS

ACKNOWLEDGMENTS

To my family, for never saying "Sooooo, when are you going to finish this book you've been talking about?" You have had great patience!

To my editor, Patrice Schmitt, for working with a newbie. I imagine you took on way more than you originally thought.

To all of the women (you know who you are), who allowed me to interview you and share your stories. I am so very sorry for what you had to go through. You are all so strong, and I have loved watching you heal and go on to thrive.

Introduction

That *ONE* relationship!

It only takes one.

One toxic relationship can change the entire course of your life.

This truth smacked me right in the face as I was sitting in the back of the balcony of a Mary Kay Seminar in Dallas, TX. I was in a very low place in my life, wondering how I ever got there. My world was spiraling out of control. My mother had recently passed away; my husband had left; I had started a new business; I was in a toxic relationship with coworkers; and I was a struggling single mother. Every moment of every day, I felt like crying. If I ever started to cry, it only lasted a few seconds, and then I went numb again.

It was the final morning of Seminar, which is when the top three Sales Directors give their speeches. This is always the highlight of every Seminar. These speeches are known for being the most inspirational, powerful and life changing of all the speeches. One of the Sales Directors shared in her speech the struggles that led to her determination and eventual success. She had started out as a confident child and adolescent. She had a good family and felt loved. She was homecoming queen, student council president, on the honor roll, and had many other accolades.

Then it happened. That *ONE* dysfunctional relationship. That one relationship changed the course of her life. She married this seemingly sweet and wonderful person who, unfortunately, turned out to have several destructive qualities. Little by little, he tore her down. He was possessive, controlling, and manipulative. He was highly skilled at mental and emotional abuse, and she eventually found herself trapped in an abusive relationship. Her life spiraled downward from there with depression and a series of negative events that included more destructive relationships and life choices. She emphasized how just one dysfunctional, toxic relationship changed her whole life. Thankfully, this was not the end of her story. She found healing and happiness, but it was a long and difficult journey.

Her words "it only takes one, just one toxic relationship" kept ringing in my ears. I knew it was so true! All the life stories of people I knew who went through similar situations were flashing through my mind. I could see all the pain of so many shattered lives. I have listened to literally hundreds of stories of women in toxic relationships and I have seen it in my own life.

I kept asking myself, how do you keep this from happening? That was the question I could not get out of my mind from that moment on and every day since. I have felt constant, internal pressure to get this message out. I want people to know the signs and symptoms to look for. I want people in these relationships to see how to get out of them. I want to offer healing to those who have escaped those relationships.

For years, I thought about writing a book. But that year at Seminar, when she said those words, I realized I *needed* to write a book! I needed to bring to light how this happens and how to avoid it. If people were only aware of the tactics used. If people only knew the Red Flags to look for. If they only knew how to defend themselves against these people, and what they did to attract these people, they could avoid so much pain in their life. If only I had known the red flags, how different my own life could have been!

I have had both personal and professional experience with toxic relationships and situations. After receiving my Bachelor in Social Work degree, I worked as a Child Abuse Investigator and Foster Care Worker. After earning my Masters in Social Work, I worked as a Child and Family Therapist in psychiatric hospitals, as well as in outpatient private practice. As a Mary Kay Director, I have listened to dozens of women share their stories of abusive relationships. More recently, I became a Martial Arts Instructor, specializing in women's self-defense, where I have encountered countless women who have been victims of multiple forms of abuse and trafficking.

This book contains stories of real women, including my own personal stories. In all cases, I have changed the names and minor details to protect those involved. I call the toxic/abusive person a Scorpion. The Scorpion can be an individual or a group of people, since the damage does not always come from a singular person. Sometimes it is a friend group, a family unit, an organization, or a workplace.

You may be asking yourself why I use the term Scorpion. Currently, the term most commonly used for this type of person is narcissist. Narcissist is a true DSM-5 diagnosis that only a trained professional can diagnose. Many of the traits that are being attributed to narcissists are actually traits of other disorders. I would like to stay away from these clinical diagnoses and focus on behaviors. The term Scorpion comes from an old fable. There are several versions of the fable "Scorpion and the Frog." It is similar to Aesop's "Farmer and the Viper." The main point of all versions is that the Scorpion has a destructive spirit. They are like a bomb, wired to self-destruct. Unfortunately, they take those close to them down too. They can be manipulative and abusive emotionally, mentally, physically, and sexually, as well as have an extreme need for control. Throughout this book, I will give many examples to help you understand the various tactics the Scorpion uses.

Relationship break ups can be painful. Work environments can be unhealthy. It is important to recognize and understand the difference between an unkind, rude, or selfish person, and a Scorpion; or the difference between a wounded or offended person, an angry stressed-out boss, a frustrated coworker, and a Scorpion. When people are angry with their partner over a breakup or argument, it is easy to place negative motives and labels on them. It is important to distinguish between normal problems in a relationship and those that are indicative of a relationship that will be damaging and abusive. I will do my best throughout this book to show you that difference.

Who can benefit from reading this book?

- Someone who wants to avoid ever getting into a relationship with a Scorpion. It is also for those who want to prevent their children from ever getting into a relationship like this. Knowing the red flags can help prevent the harm and damage done from a Scorpion.

- Those who are currently in destructive and toxic relationships. If you are a woman is this situation, you may feel lost, confused and trapped. My hope is that this book will give you the support, knowledge, and courage you need to get out.

- This book is also for those who have been victims of Scorpions in the past. You have taken such a beating from these relationships that you don't know if you will ever recover and be able to love again. I hope this book gives you encouragement and strength to see your way to a better future.

- Finally, this book is for those who love and care about someone caught in a relationship with a Scorpion. Your increased knowledge and understanding can help that person you love, to leave this kind of relationship.

In this book you'll learn:

- How to identify the red flags and avoid getting into a destructive relationship.

- Understand who a Scorpion is.

- Recognize the tactics Scorpions use to keep people ensnared.

- Gain insight into what makes a person attractive to a Scorpion.

- Understand why it is so difficult to get out.

- Find support and safe steps that will help you leave.

- Heal—mentally, emotionally, physically and spiritually.

- Move forward in strength and dignity.

I want to prevent that *ONE* relationship from ever happening so that you will be spared the heartache and consequences. I want to help those who have already experienced this type of relationship find healing and learn how to prevent it from ever happening again. And most importantly, if you are currently in one of these destructive relationships, I want to help you get out safely and lead you through the healing journey.

I know it may seem impossible. I know the pain runs deep to your core. I know the fear and anxiety. I understand the depression. I also know there is freedom waiting for you on the other side. Happiness, joy and peace are waiting for you. You really can feel whole again.

PART I

The Scorpion and the Frog

One day, a Scorpion asks a frog to carry it across the river. The frog hesitates. The frog is understandably afraid of getting stung. The Scorpion argues that surely it would not sting the frog because then he would drown along with the frog. The frog considers this and decides this seems logical, so it decides to take the Scorpion across the river. The Scorpion crawls up on the frog's back and off the frog goes across the river. Everything seems to be going fine, but then halfway across the river, the Scorpion stings the Frog! Both the scorpion and the frog drown. As they are going down, the frog asks the scorpion why he did this. The scorpion replies that it was in his nature to do so.

CHAPTER ONE

COVERT STORIES OF THE SCORPION

~The more subtle, mental and emotional tactics of the Scorpion~

When a woman is physically hit and has bruises, it is very clear that this is abuse. It is obvious this is damaging and destructive. However, there are so many other red flags to look for that are not as obvious. Nevertheless, they are just as mentally and emotionally devastating. This chapter will describe several covert manipulative tactics a Scorpion uses that are more difficult to see than a bruise.

The Marilyn Munster Effect

The Munsters was a popular sitcom when I was a child. You can still catch re-runs on TV of this family of benign monsters. All the characters were extremely odd. They were Frankenstein and vampire types living in our "normal" world. But Marilyn was normal, and like the rest of the townspeople. She was pretty and dressed in regular (non-monster) clothes. She was truly the one normal person amongst all the monster-type people. But her entire family talked about how strange she was. In their home, she really was the odd, out-of-place, dysfunctional one. But outside the home, the others were the odd ones.

A few years back, I reconnected with an old childhood friend, Maggie. As Maggie and I were talking about our childhoods, she mentioned that our mutual friend had made an interesting comment. She told Maggie, "Maggie, you were Marilyn Munster in your family."

Simple as that, Maggie's childhood was summed up. She was Marilyn Munster, living with the Munsters. Her family made her feel like she was so odd, wrong, and dysfunctional. Actually, Maggie was the healthy, functional one. They could not force her to live her life down on their level, so they tried to make her feel like she was the problem.

Maggie was working, paying her own way from the age of fourteen, getting straight A's, having beautiful friendships, and living a positive life. She put herself through college, got a great job, eventually married a loving man, and raised two happy boys. Over the years, she has opened up her home to other children to show what a loving, happy home should be like. The rest of her family is still struggling in every way, but to this day, guess who the outcast in the family is? Yes, Maggie!

Is the toxic part of this story that the rest of Maggie's family members were different? Of course not. We are all different. The toxic part is that they were abusive mentally, emotionally, and physically. They were extremely dysfunctional and treated Maggie's positive, healthy behaviors as wrong and weird.

The Marilyn Munster syndrome doesn't just happen in families. It can happen in any group and even large organizations. For example, Sonya experienced this in her work environment.

Sonya owned her own store that was similar to a franchise, but it was independently owned by her. The lines were purposefully blurred between it being a franchise or independently owned. The people at the top were extremely dysfunctional. The founder and CEO was a Scorpion, who shamed, humiliated and verbally abused his employees and store owners. The leaders were experts at manipulation and were mentally abusive. They had extremely poor coping skills, and even worse communication skills. They made Sonya feel like she was the problem. They called her difficult, not a team player, rebellious, etc. The criticisms and put downs were constant. They said things such as, "You are the only one that has a problem with this; you're just being a sensitive woman." "This is how we do it here, you just don't understand how things work here." "This is for your own good." Outsiders who looked in on this organization thought it looked like a cult. Everything that Sonya thought was not healthy with this group truly wasn't healthy. She was a Marilyn, working with the Munsters. Later, she found out that almost all the other store owners felt just like she did. They were also being told they were the only ones who felt this way. I will come back to Sonya as she experienced many forms of abuse in this organization.

The Stepford Wife

Talk about a disturbing movie! I saw *The Stepford Wives* when I was a young adult, and it still disturbs me. The only reason I watched it was because it was so often referred to in the world of psychology. The movie depicts a town that men would move their families to when they wanted their wife to be more "perfect" or "obedient." The men in the town would intensely observe the wife and get her physical appearance and mannerisms down. They would then create a robot that looked exactly like their wife. The husband would kill the real woman and the robot wife would take her place. They designed the robot to be exactly what the man wanted. She adored him, kept the house perfect, was interested in everything he was interested in, and had no thoughts or views of her own. To put it simply, they created the perfect spouse for that particular man.

You can see a similar scenario in real life as well. Kelly was a Stepford Wife. Kelly had gone through multiple abusive relationships until she met Miller. Miller was strong and did all the gentlemanly things that her previous spouses and boyfriends had not. He knew all the right things to say. He took care of her and her children, physically and financially. He acted like he despised abusive men and fought for women's rights. She thought she had finally found "Mr. Right."

She found herself becoming so jealous when he gave other women attention. She just couldn't get over the feeling that he was cheating on her. He seemed to flirt with other women right in front of her, but would tell her she was number one and those other women meant nothing. The more she pushed the issue, the angrier he became. He insisted she had a problem and needed counseling. He told her that since she had been cheated on before, she now thought every man was a cheater.

Tensions continued to grow. His response was to give her the silent treatment and withdraw his love. When Kelly went along with his lies and did not confront him, Miller was wonderful to her. He lavished his attention and love on her so well, that it was unbearable when he withdrew them. All she wanted was for him to be nice again and to love her again. She would eventually take the blame, suck it up, literally beg for his forgiveness, and for him to take her back.

The Scorpion will make life so miserable and/or punish the person so dramatically when they dislike the other person's behavior, that the receiving person (the Frog) hurts so badly they will do anything to make the pain stop. Over time, this spunky, feisty, tough woman became more and more robotic. She went to church because he told her to, even though he didn't go. She went to counseling to fix "her" issues. She did whatever he said and acted exactly the way he wanted her to. She completely stopped saying anything about the possibility of him having an affair. She accepted everything about him. She truly became like a Stepford Wife—all her feisty individual personality gone. Here is the saddest thing about the story: he really was having an affair!

Remember Sonya? Her organization used this tactic as well. The leader wanted everyone to act exactly the same. There was no room for individuality. He required everyone to memorize the answers to his questions. He would ask, "So what did you get out of today?" His employees would have to answer with the exact words he wanted, or he would call them stupid idiots. He would not actually say what the exact words were though. He just kept asking people until someone happened to get it right. It was a sick game he played.

He surrounded himself with people who he had trained to act exactly the way he wanted them to act. Once they learned how to act the way he wanted them to, he would give them special treatment. If they did not say and do exactly what he wanted, they were shamed and embarrassed at every opportunity.

Sometimes strict religious groups will intensely pressure everyone to act and behave in a certain manner. I had a close friend as a teen who was full of spirit and so much fun. She was drawn into one of these cult-like groups, and within a year's time, literally looked and acted like a robot! They convinced her that there was a set, specific way women should act and behave, and she believed them.

I'm OK, You're Not

In 1969, Thomas Harris published a book entitled I'm OK- You're OK. This book quickly became a New York Times bestseller and record breaker. Harris

7

based his book on Dr. Eric Berne's book about transactional analysis. The book presents four positions: I'm OK- You're not; I'm not OK- You're OK; I'm not OK-You're not OK; and the healthy one—I'm OK-You're OK.

A key signature of a Scorpion is their premise of "I am OK, you are not!" No matter what the situation, their way is the right way; everyone else is wrong. In the relationship between Kelly, the Stepford Wife discussed above, and her husband Miller, he was the one flirting inappropriately with women and having affairs, but Miller led her to believe she was the one with the problem. He convinced her the problem was her trust issues, and so she needed counseling to overcome her issues.

Let's return to the story of Sonya in the toxic work environment. Sonya knew her organization was toxic. They, however, did everything they could to manipulate her and make her feel like she was the one with serious problems. They told her she was rebellious and should just do whatever they said without questioning. Her superior would say, "you are the only one who has a problem with this," or "no one else is complaining except you." Many times, he would just disdainfully say "what is wrong with you?"

When someone wants blind obedience from you, this is a red flag (unless you are in true, life-or-death situations such as in combat or as a first responder). Blind obedience is what the top executive wanted, even on issues that related to her personal business. She specifically asked for an explanation for a decision that was made about her that went against all their previous protocols. She knew they made the decision as a control/power tactic. When she asked for an explanation, she was yelled at, had responsibilities taken away from her, told she was ungrateful, and that she was the problem. Her punishment continued for about two years, where the top executives shamed her in front of others every chance they could. One time, the CEO of the organization called her low-class in front of a large group of colleagues, simply because she got up to go to the restroom during one of his long-winded speeches.

After a while, this treatment will cause the Frog to mistakenly believe, "I'm not OK, YOU are." They constantly doubt themselves and become extremely susceptible to gaslighting.

Gaslighting

Gaslighting is a term that was originally made popular by a 1944 movie by the same name, *Gaslight*. In this movie, an emotionally healthy woman marries a deceptively murderous thief. Once married, he constantly manipulates her by insisting she loses and forgets things. He purposefully takes her belongings and then says she lost them. Once he has caused her to doubt herself, he ups the game. He repeatedly takes a picture off the wall and hides it, convincing her she is the one who keeps doing this. The deception continues until she thinks she is mentally ill and fears being institutionalized.

Gaslighting is a sick and deceptive way to manipulate people. This is not to be confused with deception that does not stem from intentional malice. For example, many parents mislead young children. The child catches the parent doing something that might give away the truth about Santa or the Tooth Fairy, and they convince the child they saw something else. Another more serious example is when a child hears their parents fighting, and the parents say, "Oh, we weren't fighting." This is not healthy, and I strongly discourage it, but it is not the same as what a Scorpion does.

Some situations occur like this just from one person forgetting what they said, or the other person not listening carefully. Other instances happen because of a different view or difference in perception. It is important not to label someone with gaslighting when it may just be that you are not a good listener or that you perceive things differently.

With a true Scorpion, however, gaslighting is intentionally harmful. They want the person to not trust themselves. In so doing they are making it easier to manipulate them. The Scorpion might use gaslighting in the most random instances. For example, the Scorpion might say, "When I was a kid, I worked at Pizza Hut." Then two days later when the Frog mentions something about him working at Pizza Hut, he says, "I never worked there! Where did you get that from? I never told you that." This kind of behavior is a red flag! When the Scorpion does this on a regular basis, he creates doubt and confusion in the Frog's mind, making it easier for him to create even bigger lies as time goes on.

Silvia's ex was an expert at gaslighting. They had been married for fifteen years. One time during a fight, he made a comment about how they had not had sex in their entire first year of marriage. This was the craziest notion ever. She gave him specific examples, including the fact that she got pregnant during their first year of marriage. He remained adamant that they did not have sex.

In addition to gaslighting happening within relationships, it can also take place in the workplace. Kaylee's boss regularly used gaslighting. For years it was common practice that all presentations be done in a certain format. She had suggested a newer format, but her boss refused to change. Then one day when she walked in to do a presentation using the customary format, he yelled at her and asked why she was using that format. He had recently hired several new people and told them they would use the new format. He looked at them and asked, "What format do we use?" They, of course, said the new format because that is what they were told. Kaylee defended herself, saying they had always used the old way. He yelled back, "We have never used that!"

When a Scorpion uses gaslighting to manipulate, they really don't believe what they are saying. They are just trying to mess with the Frog's mind. When a person is gaslighting, arguing with them and trying to convince them of the truth will not work. They already know what the truth is, they just do not care.

Variable Reward

BF Skinner, a famous American psychologist, discovered the concept of variable reward while experimenting in a lab with rats. He realized he did not have to reward the rats every single time to get the behavior he desired. He only had to reward them occasionally. When he did this, the desired behavior actually increased! Think of slot machines at a casino. People do not receive coins back every single time they put one in. They get the reward at varied times and never know when it will come. This is a perfect example of variable reward. In some people, this can create an addiction. If the machine never gave a reward, people would not play them.

The Scorpion will throw out a reward in a variable manner. The reward can be a gift, a romantic gesture, something very self-sacrificing, kindness, basically anything that makes the other person feel loved and gives them hope that the relationship can work. This keeps the Frog addicted to the Scorpion and always striving for and pursuing that reward. Frogs focus their thinking on what to do to get that reward on a regular basis. When the Frog daydreams about the relationship, they dream about the person only in terms of times when they are giving the reward.

Stephen was this way. When he was dating a girl, he would buy her fancy jewelry, shower her with affection, send her love notes, and a myriad of other romantic gestures. Everyone looked at him as the sweetest, most romantic guy. Then when the girl was hooked, he would turn mean. He would be verbally abusive and withdraw his love. With a hurting heart, she would tolerate the abuse because she just wanted to get that love back. In the beginning, he would give his love back fairly quickly. As time went on, however, he would take longer and longer to give the "reward" of his love. Stephen started this behavior with girls when he was just fifteen. By the time he was nineteen, he had wounded about a dozen girls with his actions, and most were receiving counseling.

You're Special

Of course, we want to make our loved ones feel special. This is a very positive thing that we need to be proactive about. However, this behavior can be used as a manipulation tool.

Melinda had been involved in a cult. She recalled how they had drawn her in at the beginning. She started out very skeptical, but the attention she received from the leader was enticing. He gave her gifts and told her not to tell anyone. He would say she was the only person he was giving this "special" gift to. He would tell her secrets and say that she was the only one he could confide in. He made her feel like she was the "special one." He had so many followers. She couldn't believe that he had chosen her to be his special one. That kind of attention felt so good.

When the Scorpion uses this as their manipulation tool, it almost never lasts. The Scorpion will eventually choose a different person, and, of course, this devastates the Frog. The Frog falls apart emotionally and will do anything to get their special position back. This is when the Scorpion can get full control over them.

Sandra's college professor used this tactic. She was way more than the teacher's pet. Her professor told her personal secrets. She would say things, such as, "I've never been this close with any of my other students." "I've never invited my other students over to my home." "I've never helped my other students like I am you."

"There is just something different about you, something special." "I feel so close to you." This professor was everyone's favorite, and she had a lot of power at the university. To be her "special" or "favorite" student was such an honor.

Once Sandra was hooked, her professor then initiated the physical relationship. Sandra did not want this, but how could she say no? It was her senior year, and this professor was head of the department and was in a position that could affect Sandra's graduation. As time passed, her professor became very mean to her. She started using multiple manipulation techniques. Sandra, once confident and independent, was now in emotional turmoil. Life became unbearable for her.

She had graduated and was now working, but continued to be tormented by this professor's actions. She honestly did not know how to get away. Sandra recalled how one day she was driving down the road and felt she couldn't take it any longer. She pulled over to the side of the road, sobbing uncontrollably. She cried out to God, begging Him to help her. Suddenly, the weight lifted. She felt a calm and a strength she had not had before. She cut off all communication with the professor and walked away from the relationship. From that moment on, she never spoke with the woman again.

Now and then she would check in with the college to see if that professor had gone back to teaching (after having left the school due to health issues). If she had gone back to teaching, Sandra would have warned them about her inappropriate relationships with students. Thankfully, this professor never went back to teaching.

The wounds from that relationship would impact Sandra and her future relationships for years!

That relationship was Sandra's *ONE*. That was the one that changed the entire course of her life. She did not receive the help she needed after that experience. She felt that if it had been a male professor, she could have reached out for help, but sadly the stigma was just too much for her to deal with. Unfortunately, she went on to have multiple relationships with Scorpions. Thankfully, decades later, she has broken that cycle.

Talking in Circles

Talking in circles is common for the Scorpion. When they are pushed against the wall, telling a lie, trying to manipulate, or wanting to confuse the other person, they will start talking in circles. This is difficult to explain because it truly is one big confusing mess.

Trisha caught Michael in a straight out lie. When she confronted him about it, he said, "Well, no, not really. That's not really what happened." He then proceeded to talk for forty-five minutes about it. She had absolutely no idea what he said. She left the conversation so confused. She tried to remember exactly what he said, and what his argument was, but could not.

I have talked to multiple people to get a specific example to share in this book, but no one could tell me what the person actually said. It makes so little sense they cannot even repeat it. The person will go on long tangents and change subjects multiple times. Gaslighting usually occurs. There are contradictions and distractions. The common thread for these interactions is walking away, not having any idea what the other person said.

They might even say, "I am so glad we had this talk and got that cleared up." It leaves you scratching your head! Anyone who has been in one of these conversations knows exactly what I am talking about. This has nothing to do with the subject matter being difficult to understand. It is all about the Scorpion trying to confuse the other person.

Going Above and Beyond

The Scorpion will do the nicest things for the Frog when in a relationship, maybe even things that no one else has done or would do. They will do things that will make the Frog feel forever indebted to them. Then, they will be mean and hurtful. If a Frog tries to address issues with a Scorpion, they will make accusations of being ungrateful. They will start listing all the wonderful things they did in the relationship, trying to make the Frog feel like a horrible person.

Margaret's husband rented a van and took her and her two elderly parents on a road trip through some western states. Her parents paid for the trip, but he did all the driving and helped with her parents since Margaret was pregnant. Being in a vehicle gives the Scorpion a captive audience. He knew this and took advantage of this. He began talking to her disrespectfully.

One night in the hotel, she asked him to please talk to her with more respect. He started yelling and screaming at her, threatening to leave her and her parents there and go back home. She freaked out. He was going to leave her seven months pregnant with her two elderly parents, one in a wheelchair, hundreds of miles from home. He called her unappreciative and ungrateful because he was doing so much and all she was doing was complaining.

She cried and begged for him not to leave. He left and stayed gone for hours, making sure she had plenty of time to worry.

Years later, as Margaret looked back on the situation, she realized she should have stayed calm, and simply said, OK- go. Chances were he would not have made it to the airport before turning around, coming back, and saying he couldn't leave her in that situation. He then, of course, would want to be seen as the hero. But even if he did not return, she and her parents would have been just fine without him.

Lyndsey had a boss who would do anything for his employees. He often lent them money when they were in need. But he would also be verbally abusive. When they would leave because of the mental manipulation and abuse, he would talk about them to the other employees. He would talk about how he had done so much for that person and look what they did to him!

Any time you hear a person talking about a long list of people who they did so much for, just to be stabbed in the back by them, take a step back. This could be a red flag. This could be a Scorpion. They also could have some serious victim-personality traits (which will be addressed in a later chapter). That mentality is not a healthy one either, so tread carefully.

Many times, the Scorpion goes above and beyond to make themselves a "necessary" person. The person wants the Frog to panic when thinking about life without them. Remember, the Scorpion is a master of manipulation and wants to control the Frog.

Manipulation with Finances

I want to end this chapter with the biggie! Every story I have heard and every woman I have talked to who said they couldn't leave a toxic relationship has had one thing in common: they were trapped (or so they believed) because of money. Notice I did not say lack of money. Many women had successful careers and made plenty of money. It is not about how little or how much money there is. It is about how the Scorpion manipulates the finances. A Scorpion knows that if he can trap a woman, or in reality, make her feel trapped financially, she will not leave. This is significant power. He will even hurt himself financially if it means trapping her.

Tim noticed his wife was becoming more independent and making decent money in her home business. He also made a good income. If she were to leave him, he would have to pay alimony as well as child support. Not only that, but his wife could work more and make enough money to make a good life for her and the children. He made a drastic decision at this point. He changed careers to a significantly lower paying job in another state. This affected her income and his. They made much less money now. He then started accruing debt. He sabotaged himself to ensure he sabotaged his wife. Within a year, there was no way she could make it on her own (or so she thought). She was trapped.

Another woman I spoke with, Rose, owned her house, made a moderate income, had zero debt, had a small retirement account, and owned a duplex that she rented out. She met a man who worked in finance and assumed he knew more about money than she did. Over time, he talked her into selling her duplex, then her retirement account, then her home. Slowly, he made her dependent on him.

Kendra's husband had made some bad decisions and accrued debt. He asked Kendra to do a debt consolidation loan in her name since her credit was better. He said that he would make all the payments. Kendra did this, and when it was time for the first loan payment, her husband told her he did not have the money to pay it. She was shocked and scared. She dipped in to her children's college savings to make the payment. This continued for several months, until she was able to establish herself financially in her own business. She ended up paying off the entire loan.

I could fill these pages with stories of how Scorpions destroyed their families financially. Every woman I interviewed described some way that their husband manipulated them financially. There was not one exception. It is just so easy to do and so effective. A woman with money is a woman with choices. A woman without choices will tolerate an incredible amount of abuse. The Scorpion knows this and uses it to his advantage.

The subtle and not-so-subtle messages a woman receives throughout her life reinforce allowing the man to be in charge of the finances. Many women do not feel like they are smart enough to handle the finances. Some feel that it is not their role in a marriage, and the man should have control of the finances. All of this is a lie. I will go into greater depth on this topic later in this book, as it is so critically important!

The list of covert tactics in this chapter is certainly not an exhaustive list. It is just some of the most common ones. If you are on the receiving end of these manipulative tactics, you may be confused, questioning your every thought and action. Please know you are not crazy! And you are not alone. I encourage you to keep reading as I will address the more overt tactics.

CHAPTER TWO

OVERT STORIES OF THE SCORPION

*~The more obvious, physical and aggressive
tactics of the Scorpion~*

The following overt tactics are easier to recognize for people looking in from the outside. They are also easier for the individual in the relationship to identify. That does not always mean, however, the person in the relationship will identify them as toxic. The Scorpion can manipulate his worst behavior to seem as if his actions are someone else's fault. Here is a list of some common overt behaviors of the Scorpion.

Ganging up

When the Scorpion is with your friends, their friends, family, whomever, they often take that opportunity to gang up on you. This is particularly maddening. It is bad enough to defend yourself against one person, but when people close to you join in, it is overwhelming. The Scorpion knows this and they get a thrill out of it. It is an adrenaline rush. For someone who would not hurt another person in this way, it is difficult to understand the rush that comes from getting others to join your attack. It is all about power and appearances. Think about the playground bully. They want others to join in and support them. There is energy in numbers, and they thrive on building this negative energy.

Sara had a friend group that would gang up on her. They started off being good friends. She felt a sense of belonging with them. They made her feel special, like she was one of the chosen few. Her family situation had not been a healthy one, and so this new group became her family. Unfortunately, they were bullies. Sara had low self-esteem, and they preyed on that. It wasn't bad if she was just with one of them, but when she was with all of them, they would gang up on her. She was the target of all their jokes. They even talked badly about her ethnicity right in front of her. When she would try to defend herself, they would just laugh and talk over her. Leaving this group was difficult because she felt like she had no one to turn to. They had isolated her from other friends, so she felt like she would be alone.

Often, the best way to handle one of these situations is to simply remove yourself from them. Defending yourself, getting angry, arguing, etc. will probably only make it worse. As you become internally stronger and more confident, these situations will happen less, and you will find new ways to deal with them.

Aggression

Aggression can come in many forms. Aggression is not just physical, but mental, emotional, and sexual as well. Aggressive people need an outlet. The anger and stress keep growing and growing, and they need a release. After a person yells at or hits their wife or children, that anger and stress leaves their body. They feel a sense of relief. Then they sometimes realize that was not acceptable behavior and apologize. But the cycle continues. A hard-core Scorpion will not apologize. They will twist it to make it the other person's fault.

When the aggression is not physical, Scorpions will claim they are not aggressive because, as they state, "I never hit you!" But they might throw something across the room in your direction. It may shatter behind you but not hit you. They will tower over you, screaming at you, or drive dangerously fast when you are in the car, back you in to a corner, hold their fist up at you, push you aside, and the list goes on. Aggression like that is NEVER OK! Here are a few examples of aggression and abuse that is not actual hitting.

Andrea's husband was given the advice to lock her in a room until she submitted to him. Unfortunately, he acted on that advice. He misused the Bible and religion to manipulate and guilt her into doing things against her will. This was definitely abusive and not Biblical!

Stacia would wake up to her husband inches from her face, yelling at her. No particular reason. He would just find something to yell about. Sometimes the aggression was more subtle. One time she injured her foot and was sitting with it propped up with ice. He said "let me see it," took the ice off, grabbed it, shook it, and said "looks good to me." Of course, he pretended he was just joking.

Tom and Susan were on a long car ride (which is not advised to do with a toxic person). Tom was irritated with

Susan. Out of respect for the older couple they were staying with, they had to sleep in separate rooms. This couple was conservative, and Tom and Susan were not married. The couple's young granddaughter was also staying there, and so they felt uncomfortable with Tom and Susan sleeping together. Susan felt it was their house, so they had every right to make this request. This meant Tom would not be getting any sex, which made him very upset.

The argument escalated as they were driving back home. He was driving fast and erratically, screaming at the top of his lungs. Susan could not even tell me what he was yelling about. She was so terrified and traumatized she couldn't even remember. His face was beat red, and his veins were bulging. He was completely out of control. There was no way for her to escape. They were still a few states away from being home. After he stopped yelling, he was silent for a long time. Then he made a very impulsive decision. He pulled over to a hotel, looked at her, held her hand and said, "we need this." She was too terrified to say no. She thought if she said no, he would start yelling again. So, she went in to the hotel with him and tried to stomach her way through sex. She did not want to be with him, but she felt she had no other option. It was a horrible situation to be in.

When the aggression is physical, serious harm or death can happen quickly. There is no way to gauge when that fatal moment could be. If you find yourself in this type of situation, please seek help immediately. Domestic violence is an all too familiar problem in our society. There are so many resources now to help you get out. Please do not feel alone. Call the National Domestic Abuse hotline immediately (800-799-7233).

These resources are there for you too, if the abuse is other than physical. Please do not think that just because the Scorpion did not hit you, that he is not dangerous. It is critically important that you get out of the situation, and stay in a safe environment, so you can begin the healing process.

Fear of Embarrassment

This tactic is especially effective against those who care a lot about how they are seen, and what others think about them. Scorpions love to see their victims humiliated.

Anne would worry herself sick before attending a social event with her husband. She never knew how he would act. If they had good sex prior to leaving, he would treat her great. But if he wanted sex, and she declined, he would embarrass her horribly. He would sometimes do something prior to them leaving to test her. One time he put the baby in the car seat but didn't pull the straps tight. They were hanging down very loose. She knew if she tightened it, he would complain about how nothing he did was ever good enough. But she certainly couldn't leave her baby in an unsafe situation. She knew if she fixed it, she would pay for it when she arrived at their friend's house. Sure enough, he was all worked up by the time they got there. Throughout the night, he made several negative comments about Anne and criticized her many times. He would say things like she never cleaned the house, even though she was a neat freak. The more times this happened, the more careful Anne became about keeping her husband happy and giving him everything he wanted prior to a social event.

The other trick he played with social events was to back out at the last minute. Manners and etiquette were very important to Anne, and if they told someone they were coming over or committed to something, she felt it was rude to back out at the last minute. Her husband knew this and would start a fight right before they were about to leave and then threaten to not go. She would beg him to go. Sometimes, the only way to get him to go was to have sex with him right at that moment. Looking back, Anne wishes she had just walked out the door without him, and not worried about what people thought.

Sonya dealt with this within her work environment. Her superior wanted her to basically lie to her clients. She refused even though she knew she would be punished. Later at a staff meeting, he shamed her and humiliated her in front of all her colleagues just because she did not want to lie to her clients.

Sonya recounted how she would become physically ill prior to a company event, just from thinking about the shame and humiliation that awaited her. Her heart would race, her chest would get tight, her stomach would ache, and she would be unable to eat. One time it was so bad that it affected her health to the point of exacerbating a thyroid condition. Her doctor put her on bed rest, and wrote her a letter excusing her from work. Once Sonya knew she was no longer going to the event, she immediately started feeling better. Of course, she had many consequences to deal with afterwards. They had to make an example out of her so others would not try to do the same thing.

This fear can be paralyzing. Learning how to stand up for yourself in these situations is critical for healing and having healthy relationships in your future.

Insults

The Scorpion is great at insults! They are experts at discovering the things that will bother you the most. If they know you take pride in your cooking and you put a lot of effort in to it, then they might say "You are so lazy, you never cook." or "you are a terrible cook." You are likely the giver in the relationship, so a common insult would be for them to say, "you are so selfish!" If you are self-conscious about your weight, they may compliment another woman's body. Then when you ask them about it, they will deny that they were directing anything at you. Some will just straight out say, "you are fat."

The insults do not even have to make any sense. Amanda's husband Max called her a neat freak one day and, the very next day, called her a slob. This seems ridiculous, but Amanda still tried to defend herself and point out that just the previous day, he had said the opposite. He didn't even deny saying it. It is natural to want to defend yourself, but that is useless with the Scorpion. They do not involve logic in their thinking or actions.

Sexual Abuse

In a toxic relationship, there is often some level of sexual dysfunction. The previous example of Susan having to stop at a hotel for sex on the car ride home, is a perfect example. Often the Scorpion MUST have sex. They get extremely agitated if they cannot have sex, and a "no" from their partner is seen as rejection. This is sure to set off aggression or punishment of some sort.

Sometimes the "punishment" is not direct. They may be mean to the kids, or say no to something they would normally say yes to, pull away financial resources, or say "if you won't have sex then I am not…. (fill in the blank)."

Gordon had serious sexual dysfunction. He became sexually active at a young age (14/15). He had been with many people over the years and always expected sex very early in the relationship, often on the first date. He wanted sex daily, and often multiple times in a day. If his wife was tired or busy, he would get enraged by the inferred rejection. It often seemed that he would set himself up for the "no."

Often, when they would walk in the door from church, their young children were hungry, and so his wife Stacey would start cooking. She would be at the stove with burners on and food cooking, and he would come up to her and try to pull her towards the bedroom. She would say wait and he would blow up! The rest of the day was fighting, culminating in her having to have sex with him after being verbally abused by him for hours. Having sex with him would completely repulse Stacey. Often when she was rushing out for work, he would stop her and want a "quickie" before she left. She would say she couldn't because she would be late and he would again get enraged. For the rest of the day, she had to worry about what was going to happen when she returned home.

Gordon was often very aggressive when they would have sex. He never made love to her; it was always just sex. He was so rough that she frequently got bladder infections. He told her she could have whatever she wanted if she had sex with him when he wanted it. It didn't matter how often they had sex; it was never enough. She never learned what the source of his dysfunction was, but others in his family had it as well. His brother was the same except instead of getting mad at his wife and taking it out on her, he got mad at the children and took it out on them.

Some men will not give their wife money for groceries unless they first get sex. Some use religion to justify that the woman needs to indulge his every need. There are endless ways a person can abuse the sexual relationship. These are just a few examples.

Fear of Safety

Nan was from South America. Many years ago, she escaped her country and sought safety and refuge in the United States. In South America, her husband was beating her regularly. Where she lived, there was no support for women of domestic violence. She was going to end up dead if she did not get away. So, she took the risk, left her country, and found a job working with a cleaning company in the United States. She worked very hard and tried to rebuild her life. One day, a situation arose that could have threatened her safety and ability to stay in the U.S. Her boss reached out to her lovingly. He offered protection. Slowly, the relationship evolved. He was her protector. He knew her secrets. He made her feel loved.

She fell in love with her Prince Charming and they soon wed. Things were good for a while, but then he turned. Slowly, he became physically abusive. One night, she fought back and her daughter called the police for help. Unfortunately, her husband manipulated the police and her daughter, and Nan ended up in jail.

Nan's story is a long one. Someday I would love to write a book just on her life. But for right now, I will give you a quick synopsis. God intervened and Nan met all the right people, and from this situation, she was able to get all her legal documents. She went on to become a citizen of the United States and her life has flourished!

Then her ex re-entered the picture. He pretended to have "found God" and to have become a changed man. They dated, and he was wonderful. They eventually re-married. Things were good until he had a setback in his business. Nan's business was doing great, and he soon became resentful of her. Slowly but surely, the abuse began again. This time, Nan was not trapped. She understood the legal system, she had a business, and she had money. She immediately had him kicked out and divorced him. This time she said she will never let him back!

The fear of safety has been used to control people since the beginning of time. That is how pimps keep women in prostitution and slavery. The threat does not have to always be physical. It is often fear of how will I eat, how will I provide for my children, where will I live. The Scorpion will learn what his victim's greatest fears are, and use that against them.

Harm to Property

Scorpions will often destroy their partners belongings as a punishment and control tactic. They might cut up or burn their clothes. They may break special family heirlooms. They might just load them up in the car and take them for donation, or sell them. There are so many ways this can play out.

Gloria went out of town for business, which of course her husband was not happy about. While she was gone her husband gave their children's playground (that had been purchased by Glorias parents), away to the neighbor. Every time Gloria and her children looked out the back window, they had to see the playground in someone else's yard. This was his way of punishing her for leaving.

This wasn't the only thing he did while Gloria was gone on this trip. He also went under their bed and took sterling silver that her mother had given her. Glorias mother told Gloria to hold on to it and save it until silver prices were high, and then sell it and go on a vacation. While she was gone her husband took it to a pawn shop and sold it for a couple hundred dollars.

Sadly, the more sentimental a belonging is, the more useful it is as a weapon to be used by the Scorpion. I feel that this internal desire to destroy another's property to cause that person pain, speaks volumes about the condition of their own heart.

The information I have presented in the first two chapters is heavy. It may have been tough for you to read through and may have caused painful memories. Some situations, I am sure, were disturbing. I tried not to be too graphic, but I think it is important for women to get a clear picture of what the Scorpion looks like.

In part 2, you will learn more about the Frog. There is an old tale about cooking frogs in a pot (there is a long-standing debate about the scientific validity of this, but that is not the point here). This analogy will help you understand how one gets into a relationship with a Scorpion and why they stay.

You will also learn how this relationship affects them. Please hang in there. You will find help, healing, encouragement, and answers as you go through this book.

Part II

The Frog in the Pot

A man wanted to cook frogs for his guests. He got a large pot and boiled water. He then proceeded to throw the frogs in to the boiling water. The frogs instantly realized the intense danger and felt the pain and discomfort. Out of a sheer survival instinct, they jumped out. Frustrated, the man came up with another plan. He once again got a large pot, but this time filled it with slightly warm water. He put the frogs in this pot of comfortable, warm water where they felt relaxed and safe. Then he slowly and gradually turned the temperature up, and the frogs did not notice it. One degree at a time, the frogs became immobilized. Before they knew it, one degree more, and the frogs were dead.

CHAPTER THREE

WHY IS SHE THIS WAY?

~The effects on a person from being in a relationship with a Scorpion~

One degree at a time, women fall into an abusive situation. If the Scorpion acted his worst on the day they met, most women would run. The Scorpion usually starts out romantic and charming. He slowly and methodically manipulates and tears down the Frog. A woman who is the recipient of this toxic behavior will, over time, develop character traits, symptoms, and responses (some of these she may have already had) as a result. In this chapter, we will look at some of the effects of being in these toxic relationships. Whether or not these were large issues for her initially, the Scorpion-Frog relationship will impact them. Let's look at the many ways the Scorpion impacts the Frog's whole being.

Integrity—The frog's integrity is often compromised little by little until they don't even realize their own dishonesty. It often develops as a coping mechanism or a survival skill.

This happened to Tina. She started lying and being deceptive to avoid her husband's wrath. It started with small things. Things that were quite innocent, like exercising. Most all people would view exercise as a positive thing to do, yet she had to hide it from him, or he would become furious. Tina didn't understand this, but because of his anger, she made sure to work out when he wasn't home. When he came home, he would drill her about her day, and she would have to omit that she worked out or lie if asked directly.

Tina chose to have a housekeeper. She paid for the housekeeper herself out of her earnings from an at-home business. Her husband, however, wanted her to give all of her extra money to him. Tina would not have been able to work as many hours if she also had to keep up with the housework. To keep peace, she scheduled the housekeeper's cleaning around her husband's work, so that he would not know she had a housekeeper. If his schedule changed, she would have to cancel or reschedule, making up an excuse for the reason. There is nothing wrong with exercising or having a housekeeper, but here it had serious consequences.

This also affected the children in the relationship. Tina would tell her children, "Don't tell your father," and they knew exactly why. The children learned to lie and hide things to avoid conflict and keep peace. They would also see their mom lie to others about his behavior. It became the norm, but Tina did not recognize this as an issue of integrity. Unfortunately, these dings in one's integrity become dents, and eventually the dents become gaping holes. This makes a woman feel even worse about herself, which in turn makes it even easier for the Scorpion to control her. It is a vicious cycle.

Depression—Living in a toxic environment where you are devalued can easily lead to depression. Stepford wives often deal with chronic, low-grade depression. They give up so much of who they are that they become like an empty shell. Depression affects your parenting, career, friendships, health, and so much more. It also inhibits your ability to have the energy and motivation to make necessary changes.

Note: If you are suffering from depression, I highly encourage you to seek professional help. There are many national and local Depression Hotlines you can call for help and resources. The National Suicide Prevention Hotline is 800-273-8255.

Anxiety—Living in constant fear of how a person will react will cause anxiety. Oftentimes the source of the anxiety is not known because it is difficult to learn what triggers it.

Samantha frequently became anxious. When she would go out with her friends, there was always a moment when fear would rise up in her, and she would start worrying if her husband would be angry by the time she returned. From that point on, she could not enjoy herself because the anxiety would continue to grow. When she returned home, sure enough, he would justify her anxiety. The accusations, screaming, and fighting commenced. This would occur whenever she was away from him. Even when she was working or caring for her elderly mother, he would call multiple times to ask when she would be home. Samantha would immediately feel anxiety as soon as she heard the garage door opening at the end of his work day. She became conditioned to jump up and run around trying to fix anything in the house that might bother him when he entered. The entire family walked around on eggshells, never knowing what would set him off.

Doing this for years creates constant anxiety in a person, lasting well beyond the initial circumstances. Women feel that if they can just figure out what will upset their partner, they can avoid those things to fix the problem. Unfortunately, that is not how it works.

Expectation of Harm—Long-term exposure to abusive behavior leaves you with the feeling of expecting harm to always come to you. No matter how hard you have tried in your previous relationships, you still experienced harm. Therefore, you expect it again because that is what you learned from your past.

A clear example is a woman who has been abused physically and holds her arm to block, or flinches, when someone tries to hug her or put their arm around her. Another example would be when a woman is afraid to tell a new healthier partner something because she is afraid he will yell at her, or do worse. She may experience intense anxiety prior to initiating a conversation, and may be shocked when he responds in a kind manner.

Expectation of Malice—A person can have the best intentions, but you will always look to question the intent or true motives. You are expecting people to have malice towards you, so your first reaction is suspicion. This expectation hinders your future relationships. It is one of the many reasons it is beneficial to wait before getting involved in another relationship. It is also a common character trait of those with victim-personality, which I will discuss later in Chapter 7.

Low Self Esteem—The Scorpion works tirelessly to destroy self-esteem so you will never have enough confidence to leave. They may even say things such as, "No one will ever love you like I do," or "no one else will want you." It is also common for a Scorpion to make their partner feel stupid, fat, or ugly. Whatever will hurt the Frog most is usually what the Scorpion will say, having learned which buttons to push to gain the upper hand and retain control.

Negativity—I've heard it said many times that we become like the five people with whom we spend the most time. If you spend most of your time with a negative person, you will find yourself becoming negative. Working on positive thought patterns is critical if you are in an abusive relationship, and equally critical once you get out of that relationship.

Bitterness—It breaks my heart to see how people hang on to bitterness. Bitterness keeps a person from forgiving, and not forgiving leads to bitterness. It is a vicious cycle of destructive emotions. Those emotions only damage the person harboring them, not the person the emotions are directed toward. Bitterness will literally destroy your health and your happiness. People will endure so much to leave an abusive situation and then not really leave. They replay the events over and over in their mind, feeling the hatred and living in bitterness.

Yes, there is a process, and anger can be a positive part of that process by creating the energy that you need to keep going when things get tough. But bitterness doesn't give energy, it steals it from you and strips away joy and happiness. Forgiveness also takes time. It too, is a process. But forgiving heals YOU! It does not mean what they did was ok. It does not mean you ever have to talk with that person again. It is a release of the negative emotions that hurt you and keep you from moving forward.

Timidity—In an abusive relationship, a person often has to hold back their feelings and words. They cannot be assertive and directly state their needs or wants. Once they leave the relationship, they often won't express themselves even though they could. They have learned to be timid and quiet to stay safe. Timidity, however, attracts the abuser. That is always the first thing I teach in my Ladies Self Protection Seminars. The first rule of self-defense is to show "attitude"—not an aggressive or negative attitude, but confidence! Walk with a purpose, hold your head high, tell yourself you are worthy, and no one is going to mess with you. This repels the would-be attacker. One of my favorite Bible verses is 2 Timothy 1:7, "For the Spirit God gave us does not make us timid, but gives us power, love and self-discipline." (NIV)

Aggression—sometimes a woman (especially if they are over 40) hits her limit and says "NO MORE!" She goes to the other extreme, from timid to aggressive, so that no one thinks they can mess with her. This, unfortunately, can push away healthy love.

Kate is a perfect example of this. Kate's mother was an alcoholic who physically abused her. Then Kate married a man who was mentally and emotionally abusive. Over time, Kate started growing more and more aggressive. At first, she started yelling at the dogs, then her daughter, then extended family members, and finally, after many years, she became aggressive toward her husband. After they divorced and Kate was in new relationships, the smallest incidents would set her off. She would get in a rage, yell, slam doors, and walk out. She thankfully realized this was trauma-based and has been receiving treatment for it. But it took its toll on her, and her relationships, for many years.

Intense desire for love (another relationship)—It is common during a stormy relationship for the Frog to think everything would be just fine if they were with someone different. When the relationship ends, they are desperate to find that person and feel loved. If this is you, and you are thinking jumping into another relationship is going to fix things, I encourage you to wait. I know if you have felt abused and unloved, especially for an extended period of time, you are likely desperate to feel comfort and compassion. This strong desire can lead you to jump into another relationship before autonomy and healing have occurred. The first man who comes along and seems to have the desired qualities lacking in your previous partner will capture your full attention. It won't matter if he has other qualities that completely do not match with your personality.

You are likely to overlook those because he is filling the empty spots.

Health Problems—We are a whole being: mind, and soul, and body. Continuous anxiety, stress, depression, bitterness, suppressed feelings, abuse, etc., eventually take a heavy toll on one's body. People usually acknowledge the effects of these relationships on mental health, but rarely make the connection with physical health. Common health problems related to abuse, trauma and chronic stress are auto-immune diseases, thyroid disorders, gynecological issues, cancer, chest pain and heart problems. These are just some of the most common, but these relationships affect everyone differently.

Recurring toxic relationships—Once a person has one dysfunctional relationship, as stated in the beginning, they are set up for multiple. The damage then compounds. A person will keep finding their way into the same situation repeatedly until they can resolve it and find their way out. This is not a conscious act. It is just how it works. It may not always be with a love interest. It could be in a work relationship or a social group. Again, this is why I continually stress to not get involved in another relationship right away. Give yourself time to heal and time to fix yourself.

PTSD (Post-traumatic stress disorder)—Years of living with abuse and/or emotional terrorism can lead to PTSD, and specifically, Complex PTSD (which has recently been getting more attention). Symptoms include many of those covered in this chapter, but to an extreme degree. Depression, anxiety, and panic attacks can be intense. For years, when people heard the term PTSD, they would think about soldiers returning from war. But any trauma, especially ongoing trauma, can cause this. I highly recommend seeking professional help if you feel you may be suffering from this.

My purpose in presenting this list of the effects of being in a relationship with a Scorpion is not to overwhelm you or depress you. On the contrary, it is to give you peace and validation. There is a very good reason why you are feeling and acting the way you are. It took time to develop these responses to what you have experienced in your life. It will take time to develop new responses as well. They won't just go away because you are no longer in the situation. Please be patient with yourself, get the help and support you need, and take the time you need for healing. And above all, give yourself grace.

CHAPTER FOUR

WHY DOESN'T SHE JUST LEAVE

*~The many reasons why a person would stay in
a relationship with a Scorpion~*

Before we go into how a person gets out of a relationship with a Scorpion, let's take a look at what keeps them there. Outsiders looking in always ponder this. It seems like leaving would be so easy, but I assure you it is not. If you know someone in this situation, hopefully, this chapter will help you understand them better. If you are in a relationship with a Scorpion, I pray this chapter helps you break through the physical and mental barriers that are keeping you from leaving.

The Path of Least Resistance

It is human nature to take the path of least resistance. As humans, we want to take the path with the least perceived pain. If this were not true, then everyone who says they are going to work out, lose weight, eat healthy... would.

But getting up early and pushing yourself at the gym is painful. Staying in your nice, cozy, warm bed is not painful. The decision to stay in bed as opposed to working out will, over time, cause significant pain, but we just look at the immediate feeling or desire. People do not see that they are merely delaying the bigger pain. This is true of relationships as well.

Shelly knew the man she was dating had some serious issues that caused her concern. She tried to break up with him, but it just hurt so much. Gary pursued her, begging her to stay with him. She gave in, and the pain temporarily subsided. Seventeen years of verbal, mental, and emotional abuse later, she and her two children finally left. She can look back now and honestly say that if she had just sucked it up and gone through the break-up pain at the start, then the seventeen years' worth of much more severe pain would never have happened.

Leaving a healthy relationship with someone you see as "not being the right person" is painful. When leaving a toxic relationship, the pain increases tenfold! The person has their claws in your brain. They have messed with your emotions and made it very difficult for you to see straight. It takes every ounce of strength and energy you have to leave this type of relationship. But once you succeed, you will be so thankful you did.

The Scorpion will usually pursue you and make promises that he will change. You must stay strong! Do not listen—literally, do not listen! Cut off communication. Block them from social media and do not return calls. Cold turkey is the best way to go. Do not allow yourself to be drawn back in by focusing on the times they were kind. Focus on the reality of the toxic, controlling behaviors and keep telling yourself you want better than this. You deserve better than this.

The Known

It is also human nature to be drawn to what we know or what is familiar. If we grew up seeing toxic, dysfunctional behavior, then we are much more likely to fall into a relationship resembling that. Oddly, it is comfortable simply because it is familiar.

Children of alcoholic parents will often marry an alcoholic. Children who were abused will often marry an abusive spouse. We will continue to re-create situations until we heal and learn to move beyond what we know from our past. Counseling and therapy are so important to help move through this process. A woman is often so fearful to leave a bad relationship because she does not know what being on her own will be like, which makes any move, any change, extremely scary.

Visualization can be very helpful. We can all imagine a little child scared to jump into a swimming pool. Onlookers encourage and yell, "You can do it!" At some point, the child finally gets enough nerve to jump, and they are so happy once they have. Jumping wasn't nearly as scary as they thought it would be. You can use a simple analogy like this, or a much more difficult one from your past. Everyone has something they were afraid to do, but felt relief once they did it. Hang on to that thought, and let that feeling carry you forward.

Hoping for Change

William A Ward wrote, "the pessimist complains about the wind, the optimist expects it to change, the realist adjusts the sails." I would never want to sound like a pessimist, so please understand where I am coming from when I say, "they are not going to change." Yes, anything is possible with God. But God gave us free choice. YOU cannot change anyone, especially not an adult. You may influence and guide, but ultimately, it is up to the individual.

In movies, the love of a woman changes a man, as does Belle in *Beauty and the Beast*, for example. This is a fairytale, however, not reality. If you are saying to yourself, "But there are exceptions to every rule." Yes, that is true. But you only have one life. Are you willing to risk ruining your one life in hopes of that rare exception? And more importantly, every day you are with that person, you are allowing damage to be done to you, your soul, your self-esteem, your very being. You must get away to stop the assault on yourself. If the person is going to change, they can do it without you in their presence.

Recall the story of Nan (chapter 2), from South America, who married a Scorpion. She thought her husband had changed. He was going to church; he said he found God; he was going to counseling and was a new person. I was stunned and skeptical. I had not personally witnessed a single person who had really changed. If you recall, her situation was not an exception. He eventually went back to his old ways when he was under stress.

People can change their actions and say the right words, but to change at the core is a different story. I am always the first person to say don't judge a person on what they did years ago. People change and grow. I too am so different from how I was ten years ago, even one year ago. But that kind of change is different than a change of the core person. Imagine for a moment, if a known pedophile wanted to babysit your children, and they assured you they had changed, found God, and were a different person, would you let them babysit your child? Of course not! This doesn't make you a bad person for not "giving them a chance." Being a loving, forgiving person is not synonymous with being careless. Be smart! There are times when you cannot take the risk.

Another example of holding out for change is Samuel, who at the age of sixteen, was showing all the signs of a Scorpion. He was bullying his friends and his girlfriend. He controlled everything his girlfriend did, but she didn't notice this because he was charming, adoring, and bought her expensive gifts. Then, out of the blue, he broke up with her. He told her she couldn't come to youth group anymore because he didn't want her there. He started sending mean, manipulative texts to his friends if they even talked with her. This was brought to the attention of his family and youth pastor, who immediately intervened. Samuel had counseling and had many restrictions put on him. He truly seemed to change. I remember feeling so guilty about not believing he had really changed. Several years later, I randomly ran in to a 14-year-old girl who was upset about a 19-year-old boy who was requesting nude photos of her. Guess who this 19-year-old boy was? Long story short, the matter was explored and multiple girls were affected by all the inappropriate things he had been doing. All this time, as he was "working on changing," he was actually getting worse.

If you are enduring abuse in any form while praying and waiting for God to change your partner, please hear me on this subject. I want to make sure I am making myself clear—I believe fully that God can make miracles happen. He can absolutely transform a person's heart. Can a person go back to their old ways after God intervenes and pulls them out of the muck? Absolutely. Can Scorpions fake being changed by God? Absolutely. Discernment is critical here. Unfortunately, it is extremely difficult to have clear discernment when you are emotionally involved. It is imperative you stay very close to God through this process. Listen to Him. No one else knows what happens behind closed doors. They do not know the pain you are living. Keep yourself safe and let God lead you through this process. Let me state that again: Keep yourself SAFE. Get away from the danger!

Feelings of Guilt

The Scorpion can use a multitude of tactics to create guilt. An employer, partner or friend may say "look at all I have done for you," and "you owe everything to me."

My friend Matt is a good example of this. His boss convinced him that all of Matt's success was due to the training and guidance he gave him. He implied that if it weren't for him, he'd be nothing. And yes, he did give Matt an excellent opportunity for which Matt was appreciative. But Matt was a go-getter and very talented; he was actually more successful than his boss. Matt's success was because of his own hard work. And his boss had certainly made plenty of money off of Matt's success. Matt did not owe him, but his boss had manipulated him into thinking he did.

The Scorpion might say things like: "After everything I have done for you." "It will destroy the kids if you leave." "I'll kill myself." "It will kill your mother." "I gave up everything for you." There is no limit to the ways they will try to make you feel guilty. Outsiders can generally see these guilt tactics before the person involved can see them. Talking through these in a support group, with wise friends or your counselor, can help you see the truth more clearly.

The Swing

Outsiders look at the destructive behavior and say, "Why in the world would she stay with him?" They, however, are just seeing the bad. On the other hand, outsiders can also look at the good behavior and say, "Oh what a wonderful person. Why in the world would she ever want to leave him?" They are just seeing the good. There is a HUGE swing with Scorpions. When they are good, they are SO good! The absolute best. When they are bad, they are SO bad! The absolute worst. They swing from one extreme to the other.

There is not a lot of time just sitting on the swing relaxing. Life with a Scorpion is a roller coaster. A toxic man can be so charming and sweet. They open the car door every time; they tell you how beautiful you are; they shower you with attention. All the other ladies think you are so lucky to be loved like that. But then the switch is flipped. And just like that, you have someone yelling and screaming at you, calling you names, manipulating and threatening you.

That is how Gary was with Shelly. He adored her. Gary constantly talked about how beautiful she was. He complimented her constantly. If he was with a group of guys who were passing around porn, he would say, "No thanks. There is no way she could compare to my wife." He constantly described his wife as "the gorgeous one." The ladies all melted over that. He would do sweet things like take her car in the evening and go fill it with gas so she wouldn't have to. He was always looking out for her.

But then something would happen. Maybe Shelly was busy with the kids and didn't give him enough attention. Maybe he took something that she said in the wrong way. Maybe he just had a bad day at work. Then the monster would come out! Sometimes these swings could be within minutes of each other. Gary would yell at Shelly and say hateful things before storming out of the house. But he would then fill her car with gas and wash the windows, coming back in all happy. Often, he would announce what he did and then make a sexual advance, assuming all was fixed. When she didn't respond because she was still upset about their previous interaction, he would become even angrier. He would scream at her and tell her how ungrateful she was—often throwing things, punching walls and slamming doors.

People hold on to the good times. They don't want to leave because the good is so good. But the bad is so bad. The bad is abusive and destructive. The good cannot fix that. If

Shelly had stayed, the relationship would have destroyed her emotionally, mentally, and physically.

Too Old

Sometimes you may think you cannot leave because you have invested so many years into a person or a job. It seems too difficult to start all over. I know it seems trite to say, "you are never too old to start over," but it is true!

Mary Kay Ash, the founder of Mary Kay Cosmetics, started the company when she was forty-five. Stan Lee of the well-known Marvel series was almost forty when he got his big break. Anna Mary Robertson Moses, affectionately known as "Grandma Moses," started painting at the age of seventy-eight. Her paintings were portrayed on postage stamps, and in 2016, one of her paintings sold for over one million dollars. Harry Bernstein, famous author, published his first book "The Invisible Wall: A Love Story that Broke Barriers," when he was ninety-six. He lived to be one hundred and one, and reportedly said that his nineties were his most productive years. Harland Sanders had a lifetime of hardships and failures. But most people do not know that. They only know him as Colonel Sanders, who, at the age of sixty-five, started Kentucky Fried Chicken. Nelson Mandela, after twenty-six years of imprisonment, became President of South Africa at the age of seventy-six. I could fill these pages with examples of extraordinary people who overcame great odds and reinvented their life in later years.

You really are never too old to start over. You are never too old to grow and become better. Time will pass regardless. In ten years, you will either be right where you are right now, or have a whole new happy life. Even if you had one year left of life, why spend it being abused. Live what time is left in peace.

Afraid of Being Alone

The reasons for not wanting to be alone vary. Some women do not feel they have the skills necessary to live on their own. Some fear being alone at night. Others think, what if I got sick? This fear can be so strong that a woman will put up with horrible treatment just to avoid being alone.

They mistakenly think they need their partner in these situations, but in reality, that provides an even better opportunity for their partner to be abusive and controlling. If this describes you, remember you can learn any skill you need, and overcome any obstacle or fear. Whatever the concern is, it is likely the situation would worsen if you remain dependent upon the Scorpion.

Stubbornness

Sometimes a stubborn streak will cause you to stay in a toxic environment when it is time to leave. A friend of mine once told me I had more "stick-to-it-iveness" than anyone she had ever known. This can be a good thing, but it can also be bad. A different friend told me, "Never be so comfortable where you are that you don't hear God's call to go somewhere else." If you are not married, there is absolutely no reason to stay in a toxic environment. When you see the red flags, RUN! And then immediately start working on healing and don't look back. If you are married, just keep reading. There is a way out.

The "D" word

If you are married, leaving is significantly more complicated, especially if you have children. When you say your vows, you are making a promise, a commitment. To some, that means nothing. To others, it means everything. That vow is being made before God and is binding. Because of this, some women feel like they absolutely cannot get a divorce. To those women, I would like to say you do not have to get a divorce to leave and be safe. Just get to a safe place! You can deal with the rest later.

Marriage does not mean you have to be enslaved to a life of abuse. If we allow ourselves to be abused, we cannot be all that God created us to be. God absolutely did not create women to be abused by men. If you want evidence of that, then look at how Jesus treated women. Christians often take verses about divorce and gender roles and apply them to an abusive situation. This is a total misuse of these verses. There is not enough time or pages to go into a long theological debate and decipher all the passages, and that is not the purpose of my book. I will advise, however, not to listen to anyone who tells you that you should stay with an abusive person. If you are married to a true Scorpion, you are not safe. Your mental and emotional well-being is in danger every day. And sadly, many times, a woman's physical well-being is in danger as well.

Foremost, you need to get out of the situation so you can be safe and begin to heal and see things clearly. You can pray for your spouse, your marriage, and for wisdom and guidance while you are separated from him. As long as you are with him, he can still manipulate you and play games. You may think you are safe because he is not hitting you. But I assure you your heart, mind and soul are not safe. All abuse is damaging.

I saw people I knew who simply tired of their spouses—the seven-year-itch, or whatever you might call it. They left and their life did not move forward. They struggled for a long time. Often, their life got much worse. The ones who left a truly toxic relationship, leaned on God and healed, are the ones who thrived. They blossomed, leading rich, full lives. They were so much happier and healthier. They became whole as a single person and often went on to a have beautiful healthy relationships later. All of this takes time. The first step is getting out.

Pride or Fear of Embarrassment

Sometimes pride or fear of embarrassment keeps us from getting out. I was so impressed with a young woman named Annie, who did not allow fear of embarrassment or her pride stop her from ending a relationship. She had been dating a young man for quite a while. They eventually got engaged. Pictures of the proposal were all over social media. Their families travelled to meet each other, had a fancy party, and announcements were mailed out. Then she saw a red flag. The most common thing for a young lady her age to do would be to fight through it, rationalize or make excuses. She would likely question what people would think of her for breaking off the engagement. Annie didn't let any of this affect her. She dumped him! I was so incredibly proud of her. Yes, it was hard, but she flourished. Instead, she bought her own home, adopted an adorable puppy, and went back to participating in all the hobbies she loved.

Crabs in a Pot

I was once told a story of how chefs cook crabs. Apparently, they throw them in to boiling water alive (sounds mean to me). Crabs, however, are excellent climbers. They have the ability to climb right out of that pot. So why don't they? Well, some of them actually do. Some say, "Hey, this is hot! I'm out of here?" and they begin to climb out. But guess what happens? The other crabs grab on to the escapee and drag him back down! The masses will not let the one with the will to survive and rise above their circumstances, get out of the pot. We all know the saying, "misery loves company."

We can see this in a multitude of settings. If you are friends with a group of people who have unhealthy habits (drink too much, smoke, etc.), and you decide to change and eat healthy and exercise, then you may see some crabs come out. They may tempt you or make fun of you for your choices. There is an underlying, unspoken (but false) belief that you are saying that you are better than them. You are ok and they are not. They then have to look at the excuses they make for themselves. It rocks the boat and makes them feel guilty. If you succeed, then the excuses they make are no longer valid. If you can do it, then they can too. This disrupts their denial. This happens with money and success as well.

Matthew was one of sixteen children from an impoverished family. He made his way to success despite lack of education, hearing loss, and a speech impediment. He became a millionaire and role model for youth. His family would try every way possible to bring him down. When that didn't work, they tried to take advantage of him, constantly asking for money. Thankfully he was able to break free from that bondage.

In these situations, friends and families don't always have pleasant things to say. Their thoughts and attitudes are more like: "Tommy thinks he's a big hot shot now. You would think with all that money he makes he would give some to us." Or "Now that Sandra is all skinny, she thinks she's too good for us. She's all into herself now." "Cindy may have a successful career, but she can't raise her kids right working that much. You just wait and see how messed up those kids will be!"

When you are trying to leave a dysfunctional or toxic relationship, you will very likely have people who do not support you. And sadly, some of those people will be the ones closest to you. Sometimes this is because you hid the bad and they only saw the good. Sometimes it is because they are being a crab. If, for example, your sister is in a toxic relationship, and has been lying to herself about all the reasons why she can't leave. And you too are in such a relationship but actually leave, well, that shakes her world. Initially, she may try to be a crab and pull you back down. Don't judge too harshly, though. This is her stuff, not yours. Stay strong. In time, your leaving may be just the thing that breaks through her faulty thinking and initiates her taking action in the future.

You can't let these crabs get to you! If you want to be a crab in hot boiling water waiting to die, then hang with the crabs. But if you want to grow, you must remove yourself from the crabs. Visualize yourself kicking them off of you and keep moving forward. Find like-minded people who want to move forward and have high expectations: people who will cheer you on, not drag you down.

My children gave me two excellent examples. When my daughter was just 14-years-old, she was face-timing her friend Charlotte and telling her something exciting that had just happened to her. It was something that Charlotte would love to have happen to herself. Charlotte became SO excited for my daughter and started screaming (love teenage girls!). Charlotte was so thrilled for her. When my daughter got off the phone, she was all teary-eyed and said, "See, this is why she is my best friend. Most girls would be jealous and upset. She is just as happy about this as me." These girls are never "crabs" to each other. These girls get it! They see the importance of picking their friends carefully

When my son was a teen, one of his friends was swimming breaststroke right after his heat. He was walking along the pool deck yelling and cheering his friend on, even though his friend was his primary competition in that stroke. He was genuinely happy for his friend and wanted him to succeed. The moms watching were all touched by this, as was my son's friend.

To have relationships like this in your life, you need to pick your friends wisely and get away from the crabs. And likewise, monitor yourself to make sure you are not being a crab to them.

Money

As I have mentioned, and will continue to mention, finances are by far the most common form of entrapment.

Every woman I talked to said money was one of the top reasons they were unable to leave. The Scorpion will do everything they can to keep the financial situation from improving, so they can keep you trapped. Overcoming this can take a lot of willpower, discipline and creativity. You may have to go without for a while in order to make it all work, but it can work!

I remember a top Mary Kay Director telling her story. She ran with her children from an abusive spouse. When I say ran, I mean she literally ran out of the door, with nothing but her children, to a battered women's shelter. While there, she started a Mary Kay business. She would walk to her skin care classes (home parties) or take a taxi, and pray she sold enough to pay for her taxi home. Little by little, she saved until she could get a small apartment. She eventually earned a car and made enough money to buy a home.

The financial entrapment may seem completely overwhelming. With good counsel and some creative thinking, you can get out regardless of your financial situation. Later in this book, I will give my favorite resources and techniques for gaining financial independence.

I hope after reading this chapter you can understand the many reasons why a woman would stay in a relationship with a Scorpion and how difficult it can be to gather the strength to leave. If you are in a relationship with a Scorpion, please know you can overcome all of these obstacles. As you turn the page and start Part III, you will learn how to get out, heal, and change your future.

PART III

The Butterfly

A little boy had gently taken a caterpillar as a pet. He put it in a glass jar with plenty of leaves and sticks. Soon the caterpillar started changing in to a chrysalis. The young boy watched this chrysalis for weeks. His mother told him that one day a beautiful butterfly was going to emerge. The boy could hardly wait!

Then one day it happened. The chrysalis was moving. The butterfly had started pushing its wings and its legs against the walls of the chrysalis. A tiny opening soon appeared. The young boy watched for some time, and then became concerned. The butterfly seemed to have stopped. The hole wasn't getting any bigger. He was worried about the butterfly; afraid it might not be able to get out. So he very carefully took scissors and started to cut the chrysalis open.

The beautiful butterfly emerged. The boy couldn't wait to see it expand its wings. But it never did. You see, it is the struggle of fighting to get out that makes the butterfly's wings strong enough to expand and fly.

CHAPTER FIVE

GETTING OUT

~How to leave safely and what to expect~

The process of leaving a relationship with a Scorpion is an emotional roller coaster. It can feel overwhelming, sometimes impossible, and extremely painful. Your insides may feel raw, but this feeling will not last. This painful process, however, will make you so much stronger, just like the butterfly breaking out of its chrysalis.

The most important component of getting out of an abusive relationship is safety. With proper preparation, planning, and knowledge, this can be done. The key is to stay in your head as much as possible, as opposed to in your feelings, since your feelings will likely be all over the place. Staying in close contact with a counselor and attorney is especially important at this time.

As previously noted, if you are not married or living with the person, leaving is a much easier process. I suggest calling them up and let them know you cannot be in a relationship with them anymore. Then end the discussion. I know this will be difficult, but please don't engage in conversation. They are going to go into their games full-force! They will pull all the punches. You may hear a manipulative, "No one will ever love you as much as I do," or "I'll do anything, just tell me what to do!" Or they may try the other extreme using anger and verbal abuse. The options are endless. This is why you call. If you call, you can hang up. If you are in person, they can keep the conversation going. In person they may even pressure you physically, or for sexual intimacy. A Scorpion is so predictably unpredictable! It is better to keep your distance. The next few days are critical. Do not communicate! They will try every trick in the book. Do not fall for it. You have just done the hardest part by leaving. I doubt you would want to go back and have to do this all over again.

Remember Shelly? Her story speaks to this point clearly. Shelly had broken up with her husband back when they were dating. She saw the red flags and ended it. He came full force after her: calling her, sending flowers, begging, charming, everything. She gave in and went back to him, then endured seventeen plus years of abuse. This scenario plays out often, and is a very good argument for cutting off all communication with the Scorpion: It decreases the chances of you going back to them.

If this is a job/work situation, you need to plan a little more. This means looking and interviewing for other jobs.

Insulate yourself as much as possible during this transition and seek legal counsel.

If you are married, especially married with children, then you have to plan accordingly, as there are a lot more factors to consider. There are times, of course, when planning is thrown out the window. If you or your children are in immediate danger, you run. Go to a friend's house, a family member or a shelter, but you get out of there! Call the police and/or the domestic abuse hotline to provide protection while you leave.

If you have some time to plan, then you will want to begin working with a good counselor and attorney. The attorney is much less likely to fall for the manipulation. There's the saying, "the person you married is not the same person you are divorcing." They truly aren't. Even in healthy situations—hurting people hurt people. Just because you may think "Oh, he would never do that," doesn't mean he won't! It is important for women to be smart, be shrewd, and be careful during this time period. I have heard so many women say they wish they had listened to their attorneys during the leaving process. Please, listen to your attorney, not your fears.

Remember, your feelings will interfere with your judgment. The Scorpion has also told you many lies, so it is very helpful to have outside professionals to speak the truth to you. I know money can be tight and you may be thinking you cannot afford counseling or an attorney. Many online counseling agencies have reduced rates for those in need. Some offer free counseling. Be creative with your financing, take out a loan just for the attorney, whatever it takes. It will be money well spent.

When you have professionals involved, they can take care of so many details as well as communicate to the Scorpion for you. If you have children, you may need to communicate directly at times, but always do so in writing via email. Make sure you keep a record of all conversations (and remember, he is probably doing the same).

A good counselor can also help give you the words to communicate when you absolutely have to. They can help you see the Scorpions manipulation for what it is and teach you how to respond to it.

Tina's counselor taught her how to respond to her former husband's bullying. He had been behind in both alimony and child support when he received his refund check from the IRS. Before signing it over to her, he walked directly into her home as if it was still his, and then he started his games. He held the check in his hand threatening not to give it to her. Her initial instinct was to be submissive and start begging him for it for the children. Then she remembered how you deal with bullies: she looked him straight in the eye, and in a firm voice said, "I will immediately call my lawyer and take you to court! What do you think the judge is going to think about you being so far behind in support, having the money to pay me, and not paying me!" He instantly backed down and handed her the check. He knew she would really do it. He knew he would be in trouble if he didn't give it to her.

You can rest assured that when you leave, whether it is a friend group, job, or relationship, the Scorpion will talk badly about you. That is ok. They are in panic mode and this is their response to that panic. They will say things like "Oh you watch, she will fail," or "She will come running back." I have found that eventually the truth comes out. It may take a while, but it eventually comes out. When people see you happy and doing well, they have no choice but to question the things they assumed about you and what the Scorpion said about you.

Terry held on to her relationship much longer than she should have. Every time she thought of ending it, she felt sheer terror. The thought of telling her children made her feel physically ill. She also worried about having to leave them with their father during visitations. One day, her eight-year-old daughter asked her to watch the *Beauty and the Beast* Christmas movie. Terry said she didn't want to watch it because the Beast was so mean to Belle; he was abusive to Belle. The story goes that he finds a gift from Belle, suddenly decides to be nice and let her out of the dungeon that he put her in. She forgives him and they "live happily ever after." Terry tried to explain to her daughter that if someone mistreats you like that, then you need to leave. Her daughter innocently asked, "Why? He's just like Daddy—he just has a bad temper." Those words hit her like a ton of bricks. She was not doing what was best for her children by her own example. She was in denial that this was her life. She was allowing her children an unhealthy view of relationships. The best thing she could do for her children was to teach them not to allow others to treat them in that way.

Now that we have looked at some important safety issues, lets continue to move forward. I know that the process of leaving seems overwhelming. But one day at a time, leaning on God, you will get there.

In preparation of your leaving a relationship with a Scorpion, you may want to:

1. Cut back on your spending in whatever way possible, so you can save money on the side.

2. Make a list of questions and talk with your attorney about child support, alimony, whether you should get a job prior to separation, who should stay or move, and other actions you need to consider.

3. Learn skills necessary to live independently, such as home maintenance and auto care.

4. Obtain information such as your life insurance policies, car insurance, information you may need to file your taxes, marriage certificate, and any other important documents.

5. Determine living arrangements for you and your family. In an ideal world, the Scorpion should have to leave your home, and you stay in the house with your children, but depending on the situation you may be the one who needs to leave, with your children. Please consult a lawyer about these actions before making any kind of decision.

6. Eliminate the extra from your life. This will be a very stressful time so do whatever you can to take care of yourself. Eliminate as much extra from your life as possible. Now is not the time to be chair of the decorating committee at your church, HOA committee member, or anything that requires time and energy. All of your time and energy needs to be focused on your children and leaving safely.

7. Stay strong. Set clear boundaries for interaction. Use your attorney for communication as much as possible and use email. Do not respond to anything that will start an argument where he can hook you.

8. Commit to "relationship rest." A common pitfall is developing a new romantic relationship before you are divorced. That is jumping out of the frying pan and into the fire. By all means you want to jump out of the pan, just not into the fire. Be very careful of new friendships, jobs, clubs, etc. You are not healed and therefore the healthiest people will not be drawn to you nor you to them. Your new relationship can end up being even more damaging than the first. Finding another partner brings temporary relief from the loneliness and pain, but can be devastating to you long-term. Even if the other

person truly is a wonderful person, sadly, your own baggage can actually turn them away. You deserve to give yourself the time necessary to heal and change.

And of course, everything becomes even more complicated if you have had an affair during the marriage. If you are married to a Scorpion, no matter how awful he is, having an affair will make things exponentially worse. Besides the moral implications, you can lose a lot of leverage from this decision, giving him room to bully you. He could have abused you for twenty years, left you neglected and hurt, and susceptible to falling for the man who comes along and treats you with love. It can so easily happen. But not only will the Scorpion torment you with your "failure," you also give him leverage in court, because he can use it against you.

9. Walk the "straight path." Many people who are in the midst of a break up or going through a divorce, do what I call the "post-divorce psychotic phase." I describe it as that time period after separation where many people go a bit "crazy," and may risk messing up their lives. When there are legal implications to your separation, such as divorce or lawsuits, your actions can and likely will be closely scrutinized. If you go out partying and sleeping around, these actions can affect your reputation and hurt your chances in court. You take away your credibility and add more baggage to what you already have. If you live your life with integrity, with the end goal in mind, then they will question him, not you.

Now let's look at what to expect from the Scorpion during the getting out phase. The Scorpion will often increase certain behaviors, including:

Scare tactics—Scorpions will say things such as:

You want to settle out of court because you won't get anything if we go to court.
What I am offering you is more than you will ever get in court.

I have people that will get on the stand and tell the judge what a horrible mother you are.

You will lose the kids if we go to court.

You will never make it financially without me.

I will tell everyone _____ [fill in the blank].

I will destroy you.

I will make your life a living hell.

These are just a few examples of the many things the Scorpion may say. Scorpions are desperate when they feel they are losing control. Control and image are so important to a Scorpion, and both feed his ego. When these attributes are being attacked, his abusive behaviors become more intense.

Lying—Scorpions will lie about almost everything. There will, however, be a shred of truth in much of what they say, and that shred of truth may convince you that all of it is true. Think of it this way: a friend may talk in a fun, affectionate way about you and say, "That girl is crazy," meaning you are fun and adventurous. The Scorpion will say, "even your good friends think you are crazy. They came right out and said so!" This is just to unsettle you. Do not trust anything he says. Stay focused on what you know is true.

Gaslighting—(As described in Chapter 1)Manipulating the truth will be at an all-time high! The accusations will get crazier and crazier. Stay grounded in the truth.

Being super nice and helpful—Don't fall for it! The Scorpion will try to do helpful, sweet things for you. You will want to accept because it feels good and you may need the help. Remember there are always strings attached. You will be tempted to rely on him for things you did in the past. Long term there will be less stress and pain if you learn how to do it yourself. If you can afford it, hire someone to do it. Then watch while they do it, so you can learn.

Talking badly about you—When the Scorpion can no longer control you, they will attempt to control how others feel and think about you. They may choose to talk badly about you because they love to upset you and have power over your emotions. There is no way to stop them from talking about you, so try to take the high road. It will be very tempting to retaliate, but that only makes negative accusations seem more plausible. In time, the truth comes out; I have seen it happen over and over. The truth comes out, and the person who took the high road restores their reputation.

If some of the negative things he is telling people about you are true, don't deny it. No one is perfect, and we all have our strengths and weaknesses. Simply choose to ignore it if you can, or own it if it demands a response, and move on. Otherwise, he will use your denial to bully and control you. By acknowledging that you have made mistakes in your life, but are working daily to improve yourself, you will overcome his attacks. People will respect you so much more if you just own it.

Instigate an Outburst—There is a very specific reason a Scorpion wants you to have an angry outburst. You are accusing them of being abusive. If they can get you to be aggressive, then they can turn the tables and say, "See, it is really her who is the aggressive one." You must be very careful to remain calm and not fall for this. Some people, unfortunately, realize this too late, as did Rachel.

Rachel put up with years of abuse. Then one day when he was screaming at her, she lost it and threw a plate at him. He pressed charges against her and used this to discredit her. These charges came up in court and affected the child custody agreement.

You will be tempted to defend yourself, but you have to stay in control, thinking beyond the moment. (Obviously if he is physically hitting you, and you cannot leave, you need to defend yourself.) Do not be lured in to aggressive behavior by his words. This is what he wants. When you start to defend yourself, then he has hooked you into an argument and raised your emotions. This is when he can say and do things to hurt you and mess with your mind. Don't even go there. Rely on indirect communications and remember that "talk to my attorney" is a useful way to end the discussion.

Lack of Boundaries—If your spouse is the one to leave, do not think he will go peacefully. There will be a full range of behavior from love and flowers to yelling and intimidation. Boundaries will not be respected. He will barge into your house unannounced, acting as if you are still together, and it is still his place. (I encourage women to change the locks immediately.)

Requests to Talk—This is a trap. Talking in person or on the phone with a Scorpion is not good because he can lie about what you have said. It is also a waste of time. No matter how much you want to resolve things, or find closure—you cannot. Your best resolution is moving on. Any attempt to talk through problems will end in frustration and confusion. Their ego cannot bear or face the truth. Everything is about keeping up the image. They will say completely irrational things just to keep up the facade.

Sometimes you may get an apology, but listen to it carefully. There will be something that gets them off the hook, blames you, or reveals an ulterior motive. They may at some point say and act like they "get it." They may be agreeable and make you think all is better. But this is just part of the cycle. Give it time and you will be right back where you were before. This cycle will happen repeatedly. At this point it is important to do your best to think logically and not with your emotions.

Tina learned this the hard way. She was told several times that she should have the alimony and child support taken directly from his account. Her ex told her that this would be a bad idea because a lot of times the courts get behind. He assured her he would always pay on time and she would get it faster than she would from the court. Fast forward six months and he hasn't paid. He is thousands behind, and now she has to take him back to court. Many women think, "Oh, he would never do that." But it is not possible to predict his behaviors. When Tina had her ex served, he called her screaming, stating "You screwed everything up!" He said he could lose his job because of this, and then she wouldn't get any money. He convinced her it was in HER best interest not to go through with this. His nonpayment became her fault! In a frantic crisis state, she called her attorney and withdrew the order. The best way around this would have been to simply not talk to him and let the attorney handle all these matters. By talking to her ex, he was provided the opportunity to manipulate her and prey on her fears. And of course, if there is a history of physical abuse, then all in person communication should be avoided.

As I type this, my heart is going out to any woman who is going through this stage. I truly understand how difficult and painful this is. You are not alone. I promise you; you are stronger than you think. This may seem silly, but I have found that this little exercise actually works. When you are feeling weak, do the superhero pose. Put your fists on your hips, legs a little wider than shoulder width apart, stretch your chest out, and hold your head up high. Breath deep breaths through your diaphragm. Then, say to yourself, "I am strong, I can do this." You can add other positive affirmations to this, words that specifically speak to your heart (such as I am worthy, I am brilliant).

One day at a time, one decision at a time, will bring you closer to freedom. There is definitely a light at the end of the tunnel, and it is a bright and beautiful one!

CHAPTER SIX

HEALING

~The steps and support necessary for future happiness~

Healing is a long, involved process. We all wish it were not. We wish it could go faster, or that there was a simple one size fits all system for healing. But the reality is that it takes time. However, just time passing doesn't bring about healing. You must also be proactive and involved in the healing process. In this chapter, I have listed several steps to help guide you through this process. The steps are intended as a general guide. You may not require them in this order, and you may have to return to some of these steps multiple times. Every person heals and grieves differently, but being aware of these steps can help you on your journey.

Step 1: Be aware of The Hole

We all have the hole. Imagine your body with a circular piece missing from your chest. Some holes are small and hidden deep inside. Others are obvious to everyone. From the moment a child is born, they go through developmental stages, and if a stage of development is interrupted, often due to abuse or neglect, a hole can form. A hole can also form simply because you are not pursuing your true purpose. Many people assume the hole is there because a person or love interest is missing. There are many reasons these holes develop. We often try several ways to fill the void: drugs, alcohol, sex, food, relationships, risky behaviors, money, success, video game addiction, gambling, social media addiction, etc. People will try just about anything to fill it, often with negative or unhealthy consequences. Even some positive options such as sports, fitness, music, service to others, etc. tend to fill the hole temporarily.

Our society is completely inundated with messages implying that the way to fill that hole is with another person— cue the Hallmark movies and the fairy tales. This is often the key solution people seek to feel whole, but the "you complete me" message is misleading and dysfunctional. Look at the TV shows and movies you have watched your entire life. There are very few that do not specifically feature a love interest. Growing up, we never think about how we are going to live our single life. We think about the person we will marry. Girls often start planning their weddings before they even hit puberty. Everything revolves around having a relationship. It is no wonder we think this will fill the hole and make us happy.

I know not everyone who reads this book will have the same faith I do. That's ok. The purpose of this book is not to convert anyone. The purpose is to help those caught in toxic and abusive relationships. I do want to share my personal experience though, for those who this may resonate with. Based on my personal experience, and the experience of so many women who I have seen heal and move on, I have come to believe that a strong faith is the best medicine and the best path to wholeness. For me, I found that the only thing that could fill that hole was a personal relationship with my Creator.

Notice I did not say religion. Scorpions often use religion to manipulate the people in their life. Scripture has been twisted and misrepresented by Scorpions to rationalize and normalize abuse and control. Even in a healthy relationship where religion is not used to manipulate, it can still be used temporarily to fill an emptiness within. Religion can only carry a person so far. Religion is about actions and beliefs, not about a deep relationship. It may fill the hole on Sunday morning, but then Monday morning the hurt and loneliness can come back if it's not a deeper connection.

What I am referring to is the love and acceptance of my Savior. This enables me to not depend on other people or things to fill that empty space. My value and worth do not come from humans. My value and worth come from my Creator. I was made in the image of the One who created this entire universe! I am significant and I am deeply loved! I have found that embracing this fact, and staying spiritually strong keeps me from making choices that derail my life. When I have not been strong in my faith and in close relationship with Adonai is when I have made the big mistakes. Strong faith can help guide you and give you the strength that you need to get through each day.

I personally begin each and every day in prayer and Bible study. I pray for God to reveal to me whatever I need to know. That could mean what I need to know to be healthy, career moves, issues going on with my children, my own shortcomings, and most certainly toxic situations to avoid. This connection and relationship fills me with peace and joy, and makes me feel whole.

Whatever your belief may be, it is critical not to ignore this hole. It is even more critical to not try and fill it with a human being.

Step 2: Consider a Relationship Rest

I know I sound redundant, when I say *please* do not get involved in another relationship when you are trying to heal. Subconsciously, you are attempting to fill the hole, but another person cannot fill it. You need to be complete without a partner. Your partner should complement you, not complete you. Before you find the "right one," you need to BE the right one.

There's this magnet out there that draws people in to the same situation over and over again until we resolve the issue. Getting into another potentially dysfunctional situation just compounds the damage already done. At this moment, as you are reading this, pay close attention to what you are saying to yourself. Are thoughts going through your head such as,

Oh, I'm over him.

I have dealt with my past. I started the healing process a long time ago while we were still together.

I am way ahead of most people at this stage.

It's been longer than it seems.

We were apart emotionally, way before we were apart physically.

This time really is different because....

The list of excuses is endless.

There is healing and growth that happens when you are single that cannot happen when you are in a relationship. Even if you meet a healthy, wonderful person, your old wounds, and behaviors from those wounds could ruin that relationship. This is why that time focused on healing is so important.

Gina is a great example. Gina's husband had taken care of the house and cars when they were together. When they no longer were together, she was left with the house, but she didn't know the basics about keeping up with the mechanics of it all. She did not know that four times a year he changed out the air filters, or once a year he had the heating, air and septic systems inspected; or when and how to change the whole-house water filtration filter; or how to fix a toilet; and on and on. But you know what? Gina learned how to do these things herself as they came up. She empowered herself! And she didn't stop there. She took classes leading to a promotion at work (with an increase in salary). She learned about investing, which allowed her to increase her 401k, open a Roth IRA, and start building wealth. Gina became completely self-sufficient. She was also able to focus her time and energy on her children, as opposed to dating. She leaned on God for her strength and went to counseling to guide her healing. Years later, she met a wonderful man. She fell in love because of who he was, not because he relieved financial pressure or could take care of things around the house. Not because he filled the hole, but because she loved his company. And he loved her independence, and was not threatened by her strength.

If Gina had been open to dating early, she may have found a man who said, "Hey honey, I'll take care of that for you." Or she may have settled for someone who suggested they live together to keep only one home. The feelings of relief might get confused with feelings of genuine love. The person she was immediately after her husband left, is not at all the person she became years later. She would never have become that person if she had not had that time of being independent.

It's important to note that during this growth period, she also went to counseling and learned how to change her victim mentality. This made her unattractive to the Scorpions. Please, give yourself this time. If you were with someone for 10 years, one year is not going to fix things. You need time. Society conditions us to think that having a relationship is the ultimate goal of life. It is not! Your value and worth do not depend on whether you are in a relationship. Getting past that feeling takes work. It requires a complete paradigm shift from what society says from our earliest years.

Step 3: Do NOT go back

Once you have left the relationship, you must be very careful to resist the temptation to go back. You probably went through hell to get out—so why go back?

I once heard a preacher say that God brought the Israelites out of Egypt, now He had to get Egypt out of the Israelites. I love that analogy for getting over toxic relationships. That relationship and that person is still a part of you. When you finally get out of the slavery of that relationship, then you must take the time to get the relationship and person out of you—out of your thoughts, patterns, and life. The Israelites could not move on to the lush, promised land until they got "the Egypt out of them." Likewise, you cannot move on to the lushness of a healthy life and healthy relationships until you get the Egypt out of YOU!

How do you do that? You must trust that the leaving was right. And enlist friends or allies to be your reality check, welcoming them to "slap you upside the head" if you even think of returning to the relationship.

Step 4: Get physically healthy

This is critically important. You need your physical health to have the energy and stamina to accomplish all you need to do to keep moving forward. A healthier mind and body will also help tremendously with fighting off depression and anxiety. Here is a very simple list that will immediately start improving your health.

Drink only water.
Eliminate or cut way back on sugar.
Eliminate or cut way back on processed foods.
Eat whole foods.
Exercise regularly.
Get enough sleep.

Exercise will naturally make you feel more empowered. It will fight depression and anxiety as well. You may have to be creative in fitting it into your schedule, but your mental, physical, and emotional health depends on it.

Go to bed early and get up early. Routine is important. One of the worst things you can do is stay up late snacking and drinking, scrolling through social media or watching TV. Just go to bed so you can get up early and feel refreshed.

Spend time in nature regularly. Fresh air and sunshine do wonders for the soul and your physical and mental health. Make sure you take deep breaths when you are outside and be sure to pause and take in the surrounding beauty.

I know you likely feel like consuming a gallon of ice cream would make you feel better. I totally get it, although for me it would be dark chocolate! I also know it takes energy to make these changes. Starting small helps. Telling yourself that just for today you will drink only water is a big step. Little choices every day will bring big results.

Step 5: Counseling and Abuse Recovery

I would ask of you, for just a moment, to take a look back at your past and ask yourself a few questions. Is this truly your first time in this type of relationship? Have there been more? Have you felt abused, abandoned, or mistreated before? Each time you have a relationship like this, there is trauma that occurs. This trauma affects you in many ways. You may experience nightmares, anxiety, depression, defensiveness, or an exaggerated fight, flight or freeze response. You may have panic attacks, chest pains, headaches, or GI issues. The severity of your symptoms is impacted by the severity and longevity of the abuse. Your healing is impacted by time, the support you receive, and your desire and will to survive and thrive. It's scary to face the past abuse, especially alone. It is important to have someone navigate the path with you so you have professional guidance.

Finding a qualified counselor or therapist is so crucial to your healing. Please, do not let money be an excuse to not get help. There are several steps I'd recommend for exploring your best options:

1.) Check your insurance policy closely to see what is covered, and where you might seek counseling in your area.

2.) Online counseling agencies have become very popular and many are quite affordable. Some offer financial assistance to those in need. Definitely check reviews to make sure you have a quality agency.

3.) Some churches offer professional counseling services. They will often have a counseling ministry with trained professionals. Just be careful and make sure you are getting someone truly trained to deal with what you are going through. Many people use their pastor. A pastor can be a significant support and encourager, but some lack the training to walk you fully through this process. I have heard the heart-wrenching stories of women trapped in abusive relationships, yet the pastor encouraged them to stay. I have also seen many times how a pastor has helped with finances, housing, counseling, etc. You need to find the right person for you.

4.) Ask for referrals. There are a wide variety of certified counselors available, and some are excellent, but some are not. Ask around and try to get referrals from people you know or trust, including professionals, such as your doctor or attorney. You want someone who is well-versed in dealing with the effects of being in a toxic relationship.

Information is often said to be power, but in seeking more information, you may find yourself consumed with all the pop psychology about narcissists, codependents, and whatever else is put forth as the diagnosis of the day. But that information is not complete information. It will keep you focused on the Scorpion instead of focusing on you. And healing comes from fixing you, not them.

Step 6: Get your Finances in Order

Since money appears to be the number one way a woman gets trapped, it is likely that your finances may be somewhat unstable at this point. It is imperative to become financially stable and wise for security for yourself and your family. Many of the stories you have read about in this book would not have happened if the women had not been financially trapped. Remember, financial independence is freedom!

There are many resources available to do this, but here are two to get you started. First, and what I believe to be an absolute must-read is *Prince Charming Isn't Coming*, by Barbara Stanny. This addresses the psychological component of why so many women feel inadequate when it comes to finances. A second great practical resource is anything by the author Dave Ramsey. The Dave Ramsey program *Financial Peace University* is taught in many churches for a small fee, or sometimes free. He has many books, and resources that are free as well. His methods are safe and proven effective. You may hear some financial advisors disagree and say debt is good, or people disagree with his personal views, but he has simple methods and resources that are free, which is important at this time. Please note that my recommendations of books and resources are always recommendations of the material, not the person.

Step 7: Focus on Personal Growth.

Challenge yourself to constantly seek more information on personal growth. There are many ways to do this, but a good start is to read books on personal growth topics. Every day, even if you only read a few pages at a time, you can put positive information into your mind. You can listen to an audio book, or download books on your phone.

You can get books from the library or listen to podcasts. Find what works for you. Your mind has heard so many negative messages. It is time to be good to yourself and fill it with positive messages. Create positive affirmations (along with therapy to help you uncover your mental blocks and old messages). Affirmations are different for each individual. You may want to enlist the help of your counselor in creating these. Here is an example for someone who feels incompetent with handling finances: I am financially savvy and a wise steward of my money, or I am financially responsible and independent. Decide what areas of your life need the most attention and healing and focus on those first. Here are some words that may be helpful to get you started in writing your affirmations. Bold, strong, powerful, confident, assertive, loved, worthy, free, whole. Once you decide on your affirmations write them down and recite them daily. Challenge yourself to be positive in every way. Take 100% personal responsibility and be intentional about what you do to continue growing. No matter what the other person did, or what happened to you, taking responsibility for your past, present, and future is critical for your personal growth.

This chapter has discussed many ways to help you heal. The next chapter will discuss changing. You might be thinking to yourself, isn't changing the same thing as healing? Healing and changing are definitely different. Changing is what keeps you from having to repeat this healing process, as I will soon explain.

CHAPTER SEVEN

CHANGING

~Discovering, understanding and fixing the Frog personality~

Imagine you are cutting your vegetables the wrong way. You are cutting them with the knife going towards you instead of away from you. Because of this, you cut yourself. The wound needs to heal. It will take time, as well as you caring for it. But it will heal. It could happen again and again and again if you do not *change* the way you cut your vegetables. Similarly, in life, if you do not take deliberate steps to change, you will continue to find yourself repeating past mistakes and entering into dangerous situations with a Scorpion.

In this chapter we will discuss behaviors and traits that a Scorpion is drawn to. This is in no way placing blame on the victim! This information is here to help you understand what draws unhealthy people to you.

Studies have been done with prison inmates regarding how criminals choose their victims. The answers all come back to this: the easy target. For example, a burglar would not target a house where there was a barking dog. It's extra work for them, and they have other options. A rapist is unlikely to try and grab a woman and force her into his car if she is with other people. That attracts way too much attention and trouble.

An attacker specifically looks for someone who has low self-esteem because she will be less likely to fight and will be easier to manipulate. After teaching Ladies Self Defense for over a decade, I can look at a room full of women, and detect traits that the criminal would be drawn to and ones that would deter him. This is not victim-blaming, it is simply understanding what a criminal looks for. I share these insights at my seminars with the intent of hopefully teaching women simple strategies that will keep them from becoming targets.

Scorpions look for certain criteria. There are a few who are attracted to a serious challenge, but most will go for the easy target. What does an easy target look like for a Scorpion? They look for someone who exhibits what I call a victim-personality. These women have a set of traits in common for most all of them. Men definitely have these traits too. There is no discrimination among people on this issue, but our focus is on the women with these shared traits, who may inadvertently attract a Scorpion.

These traits may be difficult to accept if they hit home with you. Reading these might make you feel defensive. You might even think negative thoughts about yourself. That is not the intent. The intent is to help you recognize and change patterns, habits, thoughts and behaviors that could increase the chances of you repeating relationships with another Scorpion. Please, take a deep breath, open your mind, and keep reading. Here are some of the traits of the Frog.

Martyr—Women who have repeated relationships with Scorpions often show the traits of a martyr. They exaggerate their discomfort, pain and self-sacrifice to get sympathy, or to cause others to view them as kind hearted and giving. If you scroll through someone's social media pages, it is easy to pick out the martyrs. Their posts contain self-deprecating statements that indirectly say they are kind and giving. Here are some real-life examples:

I will always be the idiot with a big heart who gives more than they get.

Sometimes, no matter how nice you are, how kind you are, how caring you are…. it just isn't enough for some people.

I'm exhausted from trying to be stronger than I feel.

I don't care if I'm selfish. I've put people first for way too long and have been disappointed. I deserve to do whatever makes me feel happy.

I hate how I still try to find the good in someone after they've already shown me in every way possible that there's none.

It's funny how many friends you lose when you stop reaching out to them first.

Having a good heart only attracts beggars, liars, leeches, the unappreciative and the ungrateful.

I'm just too nice.

I'm a co-dependent, I can't help it.

I'm sick of crossing oceans for people who wouldn't cross a puddle for me.

These statements are all pulled from real people's social media. Maybe you are not surprised? You may have seen it, felt it, or even written it.

If you are one of those people who says, everyone in my life has… left me, turned on me, stabbed me in the back, been mean to me, taken advantage of me, etc., then you likely have traits of the martyr.

Cindy was raised in a religion that was almost cult like and developed a victim personality as a result. Here is an example of a time when she was a martyr. Cindy mentioned to her husband early in the week that she was going out with girlfriends on Saturday night. Her husband agreed to watch the kids. On Saturday morning he said, "Hey, my brother wants me to come over tonight, so I am going to head over there." Instead of reminding him that he offered to watch the kids (he truly forgot), she acted as if he remembered. She continued to "play the victim" to him for the rest of the day. Cindy made little comments all day hinting at what she was upset about, which he of course did not notice. She did not mention the missed outing with her friends until it was too late to fix, ensuring that she was the victim, and he was the bad guy.

The thing about people with a victim-personality is that they do not state their wishes and wants clearly. They hint at them, and when the other person doesn't catch on, they act sullen and take on a poor-me attitude.

"Servant" heart- Some religious upbringings almost encourage the development of victim-personality, especially among women. The lines between being a servant and being selfless get blurred with unhealthy victim-personality traits. This was especially true in Cindy's life.

For Cindy, to think about your own needs was seen as selfish. She grew up hearing women say things like, "Well, I really wanted to go to the beach for our vacation, but my husband wanted to go camping. That is just so much work for me. It is so hard on me, but I'm going to do it for him." Which elicited responses from the other ladies of, "Oh bless your heart, you are such a selfless woman," and "What a servant heart." But this woman would continue to talk about all this hard work it involved for the next couple of years, when she could have told her husband she didn't want to go camping. This kept her in the "servant" role (and was somewhat passive aggressive as well).

At times, when Cindy was exhausted and desperately needed rest, if someone called and asked her to do something for them, she would always do it. Even when the person was flexible and could easily wait until the next day.

As an older, more mature adult she has had to work very hard to re-program her thoughts, beliefs and behaviors. Slowly she is seeing that victim-personality is not pious, and it certainly is not Biblical. Instead, these victim-personality traits keep her from becoming her best and truest self.

Give to the Wrong People—People with a victim-personality will repeatedly give of themselves to people who are going to mistreat them and not appreciate them. That giving could come in many forms, including their time, money, affection, love, etc. They generally will have quality people in their life, but rarely will they invest in those relationships. Instead, they work tirelessly to win the love, acceptance and appreciation of the unhealthy people, and possibly the Scorpions, in their life.

One of the most common reasons someone may choose to spend their energy this way is that deep down they feel so badly about themselves that they believe they deserve to be treated poorly. Another reason is their intense desire to win the love and approval of someone in their life, and often this opens them up to the Scorpion. Evaluating your past and current relationships is critical to changing yourself and your future. Intentionally choose to give of yourself to healthy people, and release the negative people, knowing you are worth more.

Passive-Aggressive—A woman who lives with a Scorpion thinks she cannot be aggressive, or even assertive, for fear of his backlash. She will labor over finding the right words when an issue needs to be addressed. When she finally does speak, using the best wording she can find, she is often met with rage. She learns to hold in all her hurt and anger. Over time this causes extreme anger and hatred towards her partner, and passive-aggressive behaviors can emerge. Passive-Aggressive behavior generally stems from internal anger, often towards the person who is the object of their anger (although it can be misdirected to someone else).

Examples of what this behavior might look like: knowing something is hot and letting him pick it up anyway; saying "yes honey I'll do that," and purposefully not doing it; knowing he is going to run an errand to someplace that is closed but not telling him; letting him eat leftovers that are well past the time they should be eaten; knowing what he really means in a conversation but acting like you don't; turning situations in to opportunities where you can make him the bad guy.

When a person acts in this manner, they develop a bitterness inside of themselves. They also continually decrease their ability to be assertive. When a person is respectfully assertive, they feel empowered and free. Changing this behavior requires self-discipline, self-awareness, and "new words." Often people do not know how to communicate their wants, needs, and feelings in an assertive manner. If this is you, a counselor can help teach you the actual words to say to others.

Desire To Be Rescued—Scorpion's prey on people who long to be rescued. They love to swoop in, rescue the damsel in distress, and be the hero. The woman sees this as so romantic. Only recently have movies and animated films started portraying females as able to rescue themselves. For years, storylines have revolved around the man rescuing the woman, and then they live happily ever after. Books, TV shows, movies, plays, all center around the romantic relationship, and, traditionally, the man rescuing the woman.

Think for a moment if you will, when you get into a financial bind, what is the solution that comes to your mind? Do you think of people who can help you? Or do you think of how you can earn the money yourself to get yourself out of the situation?

When something breaks in your home, do you think about who you can call to come fix it? Or do you consider learning how to fix it yourself?

When you think about your personal safety, do you consider getting a man to protect you? Or do you consider getting a weapon and learning self-defense?

There is nothing wrong with someone helping you out of a financial bind, fixing something in your house, or going someplace with you for safety. We are meant to live in community and help one another. This, however, is different from a desire to be rescued. Let's look at an example.

Melanie got herself into a bit of a mess. Her husband took care of the finances, so she did not really pay attention to how much she was spending. Melanie loved to shop and within a couple months she had incurred $15,000 in debt. When her husband saw this and confronted her about it, she was extremely upset, cried, and begged him to fix it. He rescued her and took care of the debt. Two years later, she did the same thing. He rescued her again. The next time she did it, he refused to fix it. Melanie asked several people for help before she finally got a job and paid the debt off on her own.

The healthy balance to strive for is to use your own creativity and resourcefulness to fix your problems, asking for help when necessary, and learning from the people who help you. You will gain respect from others by doing this, as well as respect yourself more.

Desire to be Taken Care Of—Traditional roles generally have the man as the breadwinner and protector, and the woman staying home, taking care of the children, often dependent on the husband. In our modern society, we have seen big changes in these roles, but still many women continue to either enjoy the more traditional roles, or feel pressured into those roles. It's okay to prefer one or the other, as long as the woman is willing and able to take care of herself should she have to (or want to). Incompetence leads to entrapment. If your husband wants to change the tire for you, that's great, as long as you know how to do it too. Look at your life and think--if my partner were to die today, could I handle everything (finances, house, auto, etc.). If the answer is no, then immediately start working on learning more in those areas.

Equally important to learning these skills is understanding why you want someone to take care of you. Many women interpret someone taking care of them as love. And certainly, that is a beautiful way to show our love. Ideally, however, love that develops independently because of who the person is will last longer and become much deeper.

Low Self-Esteem/Self-Worth—Victim-personality is often connected with low self-esteem and low self-worth. As mentioned earlier, criminals look for the easy target (as do bullies in school). They will go after the person who they think will put up the least resistance. When I teach my Self Protection seminars, the very first thing I teach is to have an attitude that portrays confidence and strong self-worth. This confident attitude will naturally come out when you feel strong inside and value yourself. If you don't feel that way yet, then you have to at least act like it on the outside. One way to do this is to hold your head high, make brief eye contact, walk with a purpose, and speak in a strong voice. Inner weakness will attract the bully, inner strength will attract the type of people you want in your life.

My favorite quote is from the book, *A Return to Love* by Marianne Williamson. This quote is usually seen in poem form entitled, "Our Deepest Fear." I could sit and read this poem all day. As I read the words, I feel healing, power, love, and a calmness come over me. That calmness seems to come from a feeling of being understood. It is as if the author is speaking directly to me and knows my every thought.

Our Deepest Fear

Our deepest fear is not that we are inadequate.
Our deepest fear is that we are powerful beyond measure.
It is our light, not our darkness,
that most frightens us.
We ask ourselves,
Who am I to be brilliant, gorgeous, talented, fabulous?
Actually, who are you *not* to be?
You are a child of God.
Your playing small doesn't serve the world.
There's nothing enlightened about shrinking
so that other people won't feel insecure around you.
We are all meant to shine,
as children do.
We were born to make manifest the glory of God
that is within us.

It's not just in some of us;
it's in everyone.
And as we let our own light shine,
we unconsciously give other people permission
to do the same.
As we're liberated from our own fear,
our presence automatically liberates others.

Please let these words penetrate your thoughts and your soul. This poem can help motivate you to keep working on changing. Breaking free of this victim-personality is one of the greatest things you can do for yourself, your family, and the world around you. You are not changing who you are. Who you really are has been suppressed from years of relationships with Scorpions and negative societal messages. When you free yourself from this, and fully embrace your power, light, and worth, then you can truly be your genuine self. Then you can love yourself and others unconditionally, freeing yourself to be open for a positive, healthy relationship.

PART IV

The Master Carpenter

An elderly carpenter was ready to retire. He had worked for the same employer for almost fifty years. He went in to his employer's office and informed him of his plans to leave the house-building business. He explained that he was old and tired and wanted to live a more leisurely life, spending time with his wife and grandchildren.

The contractor was sorry to see his good worker go and asked if he could build just one more house as a personal favor. The carpenter had really hoped his employer would just give him his blessing and let him go. He did not want to say yes, but he did. In time, it was easy to see that his heart was not in his work. He started to cut corners and use inferior materials. He just wanted the job done. It was an unfortunate way to end his career.

When the carpenter finished, the contractor came to look at his work. When the contractor arrived, he looked around the house, then he handed the carpenter an envelope. Inside the envelope was the deed to the house and the key to the front door: "This is your house." He said, "my gift to you."

The carpenter was stunned. He was speechless. If only he had known he was building his own house, he would have done it all so differently. Now he had to live in this home he so poorly built.

CHAPTER EIGHT

PREVENTION

~How to stay away from Scorpion relationships for life~

When the idea for this book first came into my mind, my desire was to keep people from ever getting into a relationship with a Scorpion. I just kept thinking how different a person's life would be if they never had a relationship with a Scorpion. If people only knew what to look for and how to prevent it, they could be spared so much heartache. You know the old saying, "An ounce of prevention is worth a pound of cure."

Had the Master Carpenter in the opening story built his home carefully with quality products, he could have had a beautiful and safe home to live in the rest of his life. The house he ended up with will have problems and cause him grief for years to come. But he has a choice, and so do you. Whether you are young and building your house from the beginning, or have had a lifetime of pain and toxic relationships, you can start over. By incorporating the following traits, skills, habits and behaviors into your life, you can build a stronger foundation. A foundation that stands up to and repels Scorpions.

Independent Thinking—We presently live in a world of binary thinking. There is option A and option B. People fight fiercely to prove their personal opinion is the correct one, even to the point of ridicule and name-calling. Problems are never resolved because the fighting prevents anything from being accomplished. Often people think the only way to resolve a conflict is to compromise.

But when people use their creative brain, and look for options C, D, E, or F, a solution can be found that is greater for both parties than either option A or B (this process is often referred to as synergy). In order for a person to create all these different options they must be an independent thinker. They must be able to think *past* what they are told by others. You may be wondering at this point, how this relates to prevention of abusive and toxic relationships?

Think about the woman who feels trapped in an abusive situation because of finances. Her husband routinely tells her she could never make it without him, and she believes him. In her mind she sees option A and option B. Option A is stay with her husband and continue to be abused, but she has a roof over her head and food on the table for her and her children. Or, option B, she leaves and is homeless and broke. An independent thinker will not believe his lies, and start thinking about all the many options of how she can leave and provide for her children.

Let's look at a woman who is drawn in to a cult. A cult tells their followers *what* to believe. The person *must* believe what they believe. If she questions what the leaders say she will be met with anger and insults and even be shunned. If she is an independent thinker, she will see that this is not healthy and she will not want to be involved in a group that does not allow her to use her own brain. She may temporarily doubt herself, as she sees that everyone else around her agrees with the leader. Then the leader shares another controlling thing and another red flag goes up. Everyone around her is following this person, but she is strong in her thoughts, realizes the dangers, and walks away.

Unfortunately, children are usually not raised this way. Many school systems are set up to memorize information, and parents often want their children to think and believe like they do. Many parents do not like for their children to question them. There is a time for immediate obedience, usually for safety reasons, but most of the time questioning is good. If the parent takes them through their thought process, that helps them learn how to process. This keeps a person from being naïve and believing what the "con artist" says. An independent thinker is much less likely to be tricked by the Scorpion. When you are an independent thinker, you do not fall for what people say so easily. You know yourself and are stronger and more confident.

Financial Preparedness—If I seem redundant on stressing the importance of financial independence, it is because it is critical to prevention. Please hear me on this: I am not saying you need an abundance of money. I am saying being financially dependent on someone is not wise and can trap you. Be smart. Set yourself up financially and maintain it as best you can. If you live beneath your means, do not overspend, save money, and plan for emergencies, then you give yourself power, independence and freedom.

In an ideal world, a child would have started learning money management and wealth building from their earliest years. That of course rarely happens, especially for women. Therefore, women must be proactive in obtaining that knowledge as adults. A woman must learn everything she can about how to plan for her own future. Set up investment accounts; build savings; buy a home; get a degree or trade; and stay away from debt. So please do not beat yourself up about prior or present lack of financial literacy or poor money management. Acknowledge you were not taught this, and simply commit to learning.

If you are single, and decide to get married, consider keeping some of your investments and finances separate. Every relationship is different, but there is value in retaining some of your independence. Find the right balance. It makes sense to have some mutual accounts, like a joint account for bills, or the house in both of your names, but I personally believe strongly in keeping some assets separate. If you are already married, you can still start developing financial independence and security.

Imagine, if today you found out your partner was having an affair? Could you leave and be ok? If they became abusive, would you be able to leave and support yourself and your children? If they were in a horrible accident and could no longer work, would you be able to step up to the plate and handle everything? Whether or not you believe these specific scenarios could ever happen to you, know that every woman needs to be financially prepared to provide for herself and her family in an emergency.

I am not a financial expert. I know this, and so I have read countless books to help me gain this knowledge. It is much more beneficial to you if I guide you to those resources than me giving you financial advice. Please note I am not endorsing any personal lifestyle choices when I recommend resources. On my website, InherPowerNow.com, I have my "favorites" list. This is a list of books and other resources that have helped me along my journey, including several on finances.

Remember, the stronger and more stable you are financially, the harder it will be for someone to control you using financial abuse. Financial abuse is very real and definitely an effective control tactic. Mandy learned this the hard way, but honestly, I have heard almost identical stories from dozens of women.

Mandy's husband was emotionally, mentally, and sexually abusive. She and her husband did well financially. They were completely debt free. As the children got older and Mandy had more freedom to work, her husband became threatened by her new freedom. He started making very poor decisions. He took a loan out against the house, and then made a huge career change. He went from a 6-figure income to making a $25,000/year salary. The abuse began to increase dramatically, coinciding with the change in finances. He also moved them to a different state, taking Mandy away from her career and all her friends. Things continued to go from bad to worse. A year ago, she would have been able to leave due to having her own career and friendships, but in these new circumstances, she now was trapped. She had no idea how she could provide for herself and her children, plus pay off all the debt. Eventually the abuse became so bad that she had to file for legal separation. She started a new career and slowly built her financial independence again. It was a long hard road, but she is so thankful she did not stay in the abusive situation.

Self Sufficiency—For years I had a Dove chocolate wrapper pinned to my bulletin board. It said, "Love many, trust few, and always paddle you own canoe." I am not against teamwork, and I do not believe in isolating yourself from others, but there is a lot of truth in this Dove wrapper saying. Self-sufficiency equals freedom. And it is important to become self-sufficient, not just physically but also emotionally.

Security is a basic need for humans, but the vulnerability seems to be more intense for mothers. This is why mothers will put up with so much for the sake of their children:

abuse, affairs, addictions, multiple abandonments, etc. Being a single parent is terrifying for some women. The thought of not being able to provide for your children is heart wrenching. Women who are capable and self-sufficient do not have these fears and do not have to put up with toxic situations and environments.

There are many ways to insulate yourself from this vulnerability and increase your self-sufficiency. First and foremost is to build a good career. That can be a trade, online business or side hustle, professional career, etc. Life skills such as learning how to use the lawnmower, power washer, generator, take care of your car, do yard work, etc., all make you more self-sufficient. Knowing how to buy a car, purchase a house, manage your own taxes, obtain health, auto, and life insurance, is also important.

The other option to learning these things is making enough money to hire people to do all of this for you. I still recommend having a decent understanding so that you are not taken advantage of by the people you hire.

If the thought of this is causing you anxiety, look at the messages you heard growing up. For example, there was a time when women were encouraged to act incapable. Depending on how old you are, your upbringing, culture, region, etc., you may have experienced this. It was common for women young and old to act incompetent, because it can be valued and attractive to men. I can remember as a college student being taught that I should act like I don't know more than a man even if I do, to build his ego. A college friend of mine, who was an amazing tennis player, recalled being told to always let the boy's win in tennis. Try and recall any similar messages you may have been exposed to.

A woman who heard these types of messages growing up will likely feel unattractive to men if she shows her competence. She might also feel that she *needs* a man. Counseling could be very helpful in working through these old belief patterns. It is also important to remember that healthy people are not threatened by a woman's competence. They actually admire and appreciate it.

Strong Character —Character is at the core of it all. That may sound strange and you may be wondering how in the world a strong character can prevent you from getting into a relationship with a Scorpion. You may even be wondering what I mean by a strong character. Someone who has a strong character can stand up against peer pressure and confidently say no. They are not afraid to stay strong in their convictions, even when everyone around them is saying something different. It is doing the right and honorable thing, regardless of the situation. Please know as I discuss this, I am NOT victim blaming. A person who grew up with abuse, has low self-esteem, and/or has not been taught integrity and confidence, would not naturally have this trait.

When I talk about strong character, I am talking about a combination of confidence and integrity. Let me give you a few examples of how it can start innocently, and then go wrong…sometimes very wrong.

Jocelyn was so proud of herself when she was telling me this story. She thought she and her boyfriend were so smart and being wise by saving money. They would go to the movie theater at the mall during the weekday. They would casually walk in as if they were just checking out the movies playing. She said the theater was very low staffed and often no one was taking tickets. They would just walk in and go watch a movie for free. Not once did it cross her mind that this showed poor character. Later in the relationship, her boyfriend walked out on her with no notice. She thought he was a terrible person for not being more honest with her. However, his character revealed that he was not a man of integrity from the movie-going days. She could have chosen to tell him that she did not want to go in for free because she did not want to be dishonest. This would have demonstrated courage and integrity.

95

Another example: After a few months of dating this seemingly wonderful boy, he asks his 16-year-old girlfriend Ann, to send him nude photos of herself. He is already a highly experienced Scorpion. He uses all the manipulative tactics. He says all the right things, "if you loved me...," "if you trusted me...," "You're just so beautiful...". If she has a strong character, she will have the confidence and strength to say no because she values herself, and does not want to do something illegal. She will not be lured.

Let's take the above story a few steps forward. There are many places throughout this story where having strong character would have changed the outcome. Let's use Ann in this example to represent thousands of girls in similar circumstances. Ann's friend told her that her boyfriend's friend, John, was really interested in her. He had seen her picture on social media. They started talking and eventually met in person. John was twenty-one, so of course Ann's parents did not approve. John bought Ann all sorts of gifts and took her on wonderful dates. Slowly, he convinced her he was in love with her. He wanted to celebrate their four-month anniversary by taking her away for the weekend. He helped Ann come up with the lie she would tell her parents so she could sneak away with him. So off they go to the big city. He rents a hotel room. She does not have money or her own transportation, and her parents do not know where she is. Then it happens—John tells her he wants her to prove she loves him. If she really loves him, she will have sex with him (or may request much worse). If Ann refuses then the "mean" side comes out. John will be verbally and emotionally abusive to her for the remainder of the trip, and may become physically and sexually abusive as well.

It is easy to judge people in these situations, but it is important to remember how character is developed. If you watch shows geared towards pre-teens and teens, lying to and rebelling against the adults is a regular part of most scripts. It's often encouraged and praised and presented as being funny and witty. Parents, unintentionally, often do not present high integrity to their children. Children will often hear their parents lie to the police officer who pulled them over, their boss, their spouse, other adults on the phone, and to the child. In so many ways, our society does not teach integrity.

Clearly it is important to look for strong character and integrity in your partner, but it is even more important for *YOU* to have strong character and integrity. Without a strong character and sense of integrity, you cannot defend yourself against the pressure or flood of emotions when being charmed by a Scorpion. Without a strong character, you can easily be swept into a dysfunctional relationship.

Long Term Vision —I am a Stephen Covey fan. In his book *The 7 Habits of Highly Effective People,* habit number two is to "Begin with the End in Mind." Having a clear picture of your final objective can keep you from making detrimental decisions based on emotions. This is definitely not natural for most people, especially in our society. We are a society focused on immediate gratification. We are wrapped up in satisfying our feelings in the moment. We focus on the beginning not the end. We value youth, not the wisdom of the elderly. We value the person who comes up with the idea instead of those who work to make it happen. Young girls dream about their wedding, not their 50th wedding anniversary party.

It is natural and understandable to just focus on the immediate, and the near future. Many women rush to get financial security or have kids before they get "too old," instead of establishing their own financial security first. They may jump at the first marriage proposal that comes along, thinking this is their Prince Charming. This can blind them to the red flags of a Scorpion.

When your purpose, focus and passion is clear, you will not get sidetracked by manipulative people with a separate agenda. You may temporarily become distracted, but at some point, their agenda will clash with your own. When they try to stop you from following your path, or try to control you, you will feel the pull from your internal purpose.

Molly's dream was to become a nurse practitioner. She was working her way through school when she met Carson. Carson was loving and charming and supportive of her goals. As time passed, he asked her to marry him, and he slowly became more controlling. He started making comments about her being unable to care for their future children if she were working. He would get upset if she didn't spend time with him because she had to study. She found herself thinking about not finishing her degree, or possibly not working at all to stay home. Thankfully, a wise mentor intervened and reminded Molly of the goals and dreams she had. Carson could not handle Molly's refusal to quit her path; therefore, the relationship ended. This was devastating initially for Molly, but years later, working as a nurse practitioner, married to a wonderful and supportive husband, she is so very thankful she did not listen to Carson, but was true to herself.

If the end result you desire is a healthy, loving marriage raising healthy, well-adjusted children, then your choices need to reflect that throughout your relationships. When you start dating someone who shows you that they have a temper, or are controlling or aggressive, you will see the red flag and realize that this is not in line with your end goal. Look for the long-term meaningful qualities like a good work ethic, sharing the same desire for children, and sharing the same faith. When you are focused on the long-term goals, you are able to stay on your course even if you have to walk away from something that causes temporary pain.

A way to stay focused is to have a personal mission statement. Take some time to think long and hard about what you really want at the end of your life, not just your goals, but deeper than that. This statement can and will change throughout the years, but if you base it on core values, then it should not change tremendously. Core values remain.

I thought about this one day as I was watching a sunset. I find that people always talk about sunrises (the beginning). For me personally, sunsets (the end) are my favorite. I just love to watch a beautiful sunset. I have seen many sunrises and many sunsets, and to me, the most beautiful colors come from the sunsets. How you live your life, your daily decisions, and your long-term vision, will determine how colorful and beautiful your sunset will be.

Strong Self Esteem—Recently, I was in an elevator, along with a little girl. This little girl was so full of life. She was talking to everyone, walking with a strut, dancing in the elevator, looking at her reflection as she danced and posed. You could hear her thinking "I am IT!" I thought, how beautiful! So confident! Then I thought, will someone come along and steal that away from her? What things will happen to this girl that will break down that confidence? As I watched her, I prayed she stays this way for life! It is so incredibly sad to me that we let what other people think or say steal that confidence away from us. Why would we let someone else determine our fate or take away our joy? It seems so ridiculous. So crazy. Yet we allow it.

Dating too young is one of the biggest culprits for taking away this self-esteem. If you think about dating logically, there is absolutely no reason for children to be dating. Relationships often lead to ignoring friends, less time with family, and less focus on activities and academics. Then, when the relationship ends (which they almost always do), the child is devastated. Young teens and pre-teens are naturally more open and sensitive and therefore more vulnerable. They also lack the maturity to handle the break up appropriately.

Often boys have no idea how to treat a girl and do not know what will hurt them. They break up by telling their friend to tell the girl. They write mean things on the locker door. They post mean or thoughtless things on social media. This is devastating, and it is NOT a normal part of growing up. Just because something happens to the majority of kids doesn't make it acceptable or right. These should be the years of playing, discovering and learning, not worrying about dating relationships.

I have worked with children in multiple capacities my entire adult life. I have observed that very often, through the elementary years, girls do so much better in school than boys. Girls are focused, diligent, and generally more mature. Then somewhere around middle school that starts changing. Suddenly, "boys are better at math and science than girls." Boys become more competent and girls look to the boys to help them. Girls stop putting the focus into their school work and start concerning themselves with what boy likes them, and how they can get a boyfriend. Their self-esteem becomes wrapped up in that quest.

By waiting until much later to date, girls give themselves time to discover who they are, grow stronger, and build up their education or career. This also allows the boys to mature. They can then go into relationships without all the baggage from earlier relationships.

Whether the boy is simply immature, has a mean streak, or is already exhibiting Scorpion traits, waiting to date is emotionally and psychologically healthier regardless of the situation. If the *ONE* relationship happens at such a young age it can be devastating. This can easily lead to a life of repeated relationships with Scorpions.

Building your self-esteem is more easily said than done. Let's go back to the little girl in the elevator. She knew she was someone special! If magic wands existed, I would wave it and make all women feel this way. This is how all women deserve to feel. Every woman has value and worth. And when a woman knows her intrinsic worth, her self-esteem is stronger, so she can wear that strong self-esteem like protective armor.

Follow your Brain—What? Isn't the saying follow your heart? Following your heart blindly is one of the biggest fallacies ever. Your heart is a muscle. When people say follow your heart they are talking about your feelings. An alcoholic "feels" like taking a drink. A drug addict "feels" like taking a hit. A person addicted to cigarettes "feels" like smoking a cigarette. The overweight person "feels" like eating junk food. Should they follow their feelings? Of course not. A tired mother does not "feel" like getting up at two in the morning to nurse her baby, but she does it anyway! It is critically important to overcome our feelings and do what is right.

Our feelings often lead us to the known or familiar—it's comfortable. That comfort makes it seem less threatening, though that is not always the case. The familiar feeling can lead a child from an abusive home to marry an abusive spouse. The child of an alcoholic is often drawn to an alcoholic. Or the opposite may occur. A child of an alcoholic will be drawn to someone who is adamantly against drinking. They may, however, have another addictive character trait. It is important to look objectively at a potential dating partner and see if there are red flags. That is why going slow is so important: go slow and use your brain as opposed to going fast and using your feelings.

A sexual relationship emphasizes feelings, and that level of intimacy creates a soul tie to your partner. Your judgment becomes even more clouded, hence the saying "love is blind." So many people jump into a sexual relationship when they do not even really know the person. Instead of using your feelings and sex drive, use your brain. Take notice of how this person is with their friends, their parents, children and even workers you encounter day-to-day. Get to know them as a friend. Remember, feelings are just that—feelings. Pay attention to them, but don't be ruled by them.

Self-Defense—I cannot finish out this chapter without recommending taking self-defense courses. I personally have been teaching self-defense classes for over a decade. This is one of my strongest passions. There is so much a woman, even a very small woman, can do to protect herself from ever being attacked. When I teach my classes there is always this soft voice in my head saying, "just one less victim, one less victim."

Being able to defend yourself physically has a strong psychological effect that impacts all other areas of your life. If a woman goes through life feeling physically weak and unable to fight off a man if he tried to hurt her, that vulnerability carries into other areas. She may not state her needs assertively. She may allow men to cross boundaries at work or in her personal life. She may even think she is not as capable as a man to handle finances. But when she feels physically capable and strong, she finds herself feeling capable in other areas as well.

I love seeing a woman's face when she learns a simple self-defense technique and the realization hits her that she can defend herself from a man. There is instant empowerment. She immediately stands taller and is more confident. As her knowledge of self-defense grows so does her internal strength. I find it difficult to express how differently you feel on the inside when you have the ability and knowledge to defend yourself on the outside, but I encourage YOU to find out!

CHAPTER NINE

MOVING ON

~Living free, healthy, and happy~

You have grown so much. You left the Scorpion and you have worked on healing and changing. Now you can choose to let go of the past, take 100% responsibility, and move forward. You get to decide *WHO* you want to be and *WHAT* your life will look like. This is the exciting part!

Let's begin by looking at *who* you want to be. Here is a list of character and personality traits to get you thinking.

Honest	Spiritual
Overbearing	Loving
Alcoholic	Positive
Encourager	Helpful
Fun	Negative
Wise	Sincere
Hot tempered	Grouchy
Abusive	Adventurous
Liar	Sickly
Mean	Lazy
Partyer	Energetic
Critical	Loner
Manipulative	Loyal
Supportive	Faithful
Kind	Stressed
Role model	Happy
Generous	Healthy

This list is intended to get you started in thinking about who you are and who you want to be. You get to decide who YOU want to be! You are no longer held back by someone else. You can decide what kind of person you want to be and what type of qualities you want to have. What do you want your children to say about you? What would you want said at your eulogy? Really think about it. What would you want people to remember about you?

This is not about becoming someone you are not. It is about becoming the best you that you can be. It is about breaking through all the muck of your life and rising up in to your full beauty.

I use the lotus flower as my logo for my ministry teaching women self-defense, particularly victims of trafficking and at-risk populations. The lotus flower blooms out of swampy, dirty water. In spite of where it comes from, it rises up to be a beautiful flower. This is a perfect reminder to all of us that we too can rise up into our full glory!

Once you have a clear vision of who you want to be, then you can start working on being or becoming that person. Much of the work will be about changing habits. Some will require deep soul searching and healing. Remember, this process is not about changing who you really are. It is about getting back to who you really are—your true self.

By focusing on your growth, you stop focusing on the Scorpion. There is no need to focus on him any longer—you have moved on. Be strong and disciplined. Focus on what is healthy. Likely you have spent significant amounts of time rehashing all the unhealthy events. Now it is time to immerse yourself in the healthy.

So, what is healthy? That seems like a silly question, but if you have not experienced healthy, then you may not know what it looks like.

A healthy environment:

1. Encourages independent thinking.

2. Ideas are listened to and respected, even if the person disagrees.

3. Allows growth.

4. Allows independence.

5. Acknowledges the good things you have done.

6. Gossip is frowned upon.

7. Honest feedback and praise are given.

8. There is trust.

9. Each person focuses on self-improvement.

10. Having friends is encouraged.

11. Honesty.

12. Mutual care comes from love, not guilt.

13. Allows the freedom to be human.

14. Respects each other's bodies and belongings.

15. Protects each other's feelings and vulnerabilities.

Obviously, these are key areas to get you started. There is so much more. It is natural for a person, as they read through this list, to think about how others in their life do or do not do these things. It is more difficult (but much more important) to think about how you can create this environment for yourself. When you create this environment, you will draw healthier people to you. Please remember though, no relationship or person is perfect. Healthy relationships do not just happen. They are something that require consistent effort and nurturing.

So how do we learn how to be healthy and incorporate the attributes on this list if we did not grow up seeing them in our environment? It definitely takes time and effort!

1. As I mentioned many times throughout this book, get a great counselor. It is so important to have someone guide you through your journey. Please do not look to TV, social media, or the movies for answers. Those relationships are dysfunctional, or fake, or both! On social media you are only seeing the highlight reel. The couple may actually have a good solid relationship, but it is still just the highlight reel.

2. Read. Replace social media and TV time with reading. Read everything you can put your hands on that will help you grow and become a healthier person. If you do not like to read utilize audiobooks and podcasts. Fill your brain with positive healthy messages.

3. Find couples whose relationships you admire and observe them. Pay close attention to how they handle situations. In my experience, the happiest and healthiest marriages I have found are the ones where the couple has a unified mission that is bigger than themselves. Maybe they start a homeless ministry together, or go to a poverty-stricken country to be missionaries, or commit to helping a certain organization. Whatever it may be, when two people are not just thinking about themselves, but have the ability to think about others, they make better partners. When both people are individually healthy, kind, and respectful, and treat their partner that way, they create a beautiful relationship.

4. Practice. Practice responding to life in a healthy way. We of course want healthy people in our lives. Healthy people also want healthy people in their lives. The more you practice

healthy communication and responses, the healthier the people you attract will be. Pay attention to how you are responding. For example, if a person criticizes you, do you go off on them or get devastated by their words? If someone on social media makes a statement you disagree with, do you find yourself super agitated and giving that person a piece of your mind? Healthy would be looking at the criticism and evaluating its validity honestly. You might start to hear yourself say things like, "Thank you for your feedback. I will take that under consideration." or "Yes, I am stubborn and speak my mind." I kind of like that about myself." There are so many ways you can respond. Becoming comfortable with the healthier responses is a matter of exposure. This is where books on communication (and seeing a counselor) can come in handy. I learned the best techniques from my years in Mary Kay. I am old enough to have actually heard her in person, and saw first-hand her wisdom. I highly recommend any book that she has written. I also recommend the book *How to Win Friends and Influence People in the Digital Age*, by Dale Carnegie and associates. Specific words are given to reply to people. Your counselor can also help you find the words to say, and new ways to handle situations. But you must put those lessons into action. This is a long process so try not to get frustrated with yourself. Just keep moving forward and giving yourself grace.

5. Live your life from a place of principles. As I said before, people tend to focus on finding the right one, instead of BEING the right one! Spend the time and energy it takes to heal and grow, and be the very best you that you can be.

6. Realize that the goal of your time spent on this earth is not to be in a romantic relationship. You can choose to be single and have a wonderful, purpose driven life.

I have two more women I would like to tell you about. They each handled being alone very differently, and who they became afterwards was also very different.

The first is Lynn. Lynn's husband left her for another woman shortly after she had her third child. The girls were twelve, ten, and one when he left. His leaving was actually a positive event because he was extremely dysfunctional. Lynn however could not move forward. She spent the next several years trying to convince him to come back, crying to her older daughters about how sad and hurt she was, and walking around depressed and full of self-pity. Her girls became angry with her for not moving on and for being an emotionally absent mother to them. Three years after the divorce, Lynn started going to a divorce recovery group. She met a man who was more than willing to lend his shoulder for her to cry on. She allowed him to take care of her needs, even to the point of buying her a car.

Her daughters never had the opportunity to see their mother's strength. They never saw her rise up and make a life for herself or for them. Lynn remarried before ever letting go, healing, and moving on from the pain of her previous relationship.

Lynn did not put in the work necessary for herself to heal and overcome her past. She walked into a new chapter of the same story, instead of creating a new one.

The second woman is Deborah. When Deborah's husband left, she sat down in the recliner, looked around the house, took a deep sigh, and thought *peace*. She finally had peace. Deborah had no idea what she was going to do next, how she would pay the bills, take care of the house, and hold their family together, but that was ok. For the moment, she had peace. Deborah dug deep inside of herself for strength (which she now knows was God, helping her every step of the way). She opened up a business and made it work. There was no option of failing, so she fought to make it work. She borrowed money to pay for an attorney to handle the separation agreement. She went to counseling and rebuilt her shattered self-esteem. She learned how to take care of the house, car, and finances. Before her husband walked out the door, he told her she could never make it without him. Deborah was determined to prove him wrong. And she did!

It didn't happen overnight. Deborah suffered from so many years with him. Publicly she was managing just fine, but once alone, often in her car, heaviness would come over her and she would feel her emotions well up. But she never cried. This feeling came over her every time she got in the car. This went on for well over a year. Then, one day as she was driving down the road, she suddenly realized she didn't feel like crying! She was so happy she actually started to cry, but this time it was tears of joy, not of sadness. Deborah fought hard and overcame. She reinvented a life for herself and her children. She moved on and was completely happy and successful as a single woman. Deborah did the work and overcame her past, and so can you.

I know I have given you a lot of information to digest. This is not a book to read in one sitting and then set aside. Depending on where you are in your journey, you may need to sit with a specific chapter for a while, and that is ok, as long as you keep moving. The exciting part of this journey is that *you* can choose to build your life how *you* want it to be.

Your life is the house in the story of the Master Carpenter. You are ALWAYS building your house. Every decision you make, you are hammering a nail, pouring concrete, framing a door...

This carpenter did not build his house the best he could. But he has the option of tearing it down, keeping the materials he likes, adding new materials, and rebuilding his home. You can do this too. You can take out what is not healthy in your environment and within yourself. You can rebuild with integrity and more wisdom. You can add in healthy behaviors, better decisions, love and peace. You can put forth the effort to build a masterpiece! Build yourself a strong beautiful home.

I personally had a favorite song during this rebuilding time. The lyrics were so healing and freeing to me. Please read them slowly and let them sink in to your soul. Better yet, look it up online and read the words as you listen to the song.

Tell your Heart to Beat Again

By Danny Gokey

You're shattered, like you've never been before
The life you knew, in a thousand pieces on the floor
And words fall short in times like these, when this world
drives you to your knees
You think you're never gonna get back, to the you that
used to be

Tell your heart to beat again
Close your eyes and breathe it in
Let the shadows fall away
Step into the light of grace
Yesterday's a closing door
You don't live there anymore
Say goodbye to where you've been
And tell your heart to beat again

Beginning, just let that word wash over you

It's alright now, love's healing hands have pulled you
through

So get back up, take step one, leave the darkness,
feel the sun
'Cause your story's far from over and your journey's
just begun

Refrain

Let every heartbreak and every scar
Be a picture that reminds you who has carried you this far
'Cause love sees farther than you ever could
In this moment heaven's working, everything for your
good

Tell your heart to beat again
Close your eyes and breathe it in
Let the shadows fall away
Step into the light of grace
Yesterday's a closing door
You don't live there anymore
Say goodbye to where you've been
And tell your heart to beat again

To this day when I listen to this song, I feel a sense of freedom and I get teary eyed. It warms my soul. You truly can move on from your past and build a beautiful future. Just keep moving forward, every day, in every way. A little at a time, and one day you will be talking to someone who is in the midst of a relationship with a Scorpion. You will be encouraging them and giving them advice. And then suddenly it will hit you, just how far you have come. You are no longer a Frog—you are a Queen!

Final Thoughts

I feel this is a good time to be completely transparent. I have an agenda. I see this incredible army of change agents, peace makers, and fighters for justice. I see incredible, brilliant, strong, wise women who could infuse life and love into our broken world. Women who could portray to hurting people, the true beauty of our Heavenly Father, our Savior, and the Holy Spirit. But where are they? They are held back in every way possible. They have been put in a box; into a role they must perform. They have been treated as weaker and less intelligent. They have been lured into brothels for a life of slavery. They have been stripped of their jobs and influence and forced to stay at home. They have been told to ignore the Holy Spirit and instead listen to a man, a human being, for their guidance. They have been put under a glass ceiling. They have been made into objects for sexual pleasure. They have been raped and abused. They have been the Frog stung by the Scorpion, and the Frog in boiling water.

I see so many girls and young women with hearts full of passion for the hurting of this world. They are full of love and kindness. But then, little by little, one degree at a time, that gets pushed deep inside of them. The abuse from relationships with Scorpions hardens that love and stifles the passion and creative spirit. All their focus and energy goes into fixing the relationship, and eventually surviving the relationship.

Imagine for a moment, a world where young women, when they saw a red flag, immediately knew it was a red flag, and chose to walk the other way. A world where all that love, creativity and passion were not stifled, but released into the world by women who listened to Adonai's voice, fully felt the grace and love from their Savior, and were filled with the power of the Holy Spirit. Imagine those women in positions of power in our local, state, and federal governments. Imagine these free women running corporations, working in law enforcement, building Non-Profits, becoming leaders in education, raising emotionally healthy children, and acting as spiritual mentors and leaders. This type of world: this is my dream.

Little by little, one degree at a time, women can be freed. This book is one small part of that. By freeing women from the chains of these relationships, they can be released to bring beauty, peace, love, compassion, grace, justice, and strength into our broken world. And yes, *you* are one of these women!

I have prayed my way through the writing of this book. Now I pray for each and every person who holds this book and reads these words. I pray that you be released from the pain and bondage of the demeaning and devaluing messages and lies you've been told, which have been holding you back. I pray you find your true power and strength, and enjoy peace and many blessings. Above all, I pray the greatness in you would be released on everyone around you, and this world would become a brighter and better place because you are free to be fully you.

Many blessings on you and your journey!

ABOUT THE AUTHOR

Stephanie Jenkins is an advocate for women and children, modern day abolitionist, and martial artist specializing in women's self-defense. She is passionate about freeing women from the societal, cultural, traditional, interpersonal, and spiritual bondage that holds them back.

Stephanie has a Master of Social Work degree. She has worked as a child abuse investigator, child and family therapist in psychiatric hospitals, and a therapist in an outpatient clinic. She has spent decades working with women and listening to their stories. Stephanie currently teaches women's self-defense classes and founded Inher Power, which focuses on teaching self-defense to victims of trafficking and at-risk women and children.

Stephanie is a nature loving health nut, who loves hiking, kayaking and biking, but most of all loves to spend time with her family.

NOTES

Chapter 1

1- Thomas A. Harris, M.D., *"I'm OK, You're OK"* (Harper and Row, 1969), developed from multiple articles on this topic.
2- B.F. Skinner, (Developed from multiple articles and books on the psychiatrist and his behavioral theories and experiments).

Chapter 4

1- Wikipedia contributors, "Mary Kay Ash," *Wikipedia, The Free Encyclopedia*, https://en.wikipedia.org/w/index.php?title=Mary_Kay_Ash&oldid=1049796627 (accessed November 1, 2021).
2- Wikipedia contributors, "Stan Lee," *Wikipedia, The Free Encyclopedia*, https://en.wikipedia.org/w/index.php?title=Stan_Lee&oldid=1046796802 (accessed November 1, 2021).
3- Wikipedia contributors, "Grandma Moses," *Wikipedia, The Free Encyclopedia*, https://en.wikipedia.org/w/index.php?title=Grandma_Moses&oldid=1044924149 (accessed November 1, 2021).
4- Wikipedia contributors, "Harry Bernstein," *Wikipedia, The Free Encyclopedia*, https://en.wikipedia.org/w/index.php?title=Harry_Bernstein&oldid=1049982826 (accessed November 1, 2021).
5- Wikipedia contributors, "Colonel Sanders," *Wikipedia, The Free Encyclopedia*, https://en.wikipedia.org/w/index.

php?title=Colonel_Sanders&oldid=1050484264 (accessed November 1, 2021).

6- Wikipedia contributors, "Nelson Mandela," *Wikipedia, The Free Encyclopedia*, https://en.wikipedia.org/w/index. php?title=Nelson_Mandela&oldid=1053039273 (accessed November 1, 2021).

Chapter 7

1- Marianne Williamson, *"A Return to Love"* (Harper Perennial, 1993).

Chapter 8

1- Stephen Covey, *"The 7 Habits of Highly Effective People"* (Free Press; Revised edition 2004).

RED FLAGS